PORTUGAL TRAVEL GUIDE

The Most Complete Pocket Guide |
Discover Portugal's History, Art, Culture
and Hidden Gems to Plan an
Unforgettable Trip

D1518695

Daniel N. Martin

Table of Contents

Introduction

Welcome to Portugal, a charming and diverse country located on the western coast of Europe. Portugal is a country with a rich history and culture, breathtaking landscapes, delicious cuisine, and warm and welcoming people. From the vibrant cities of Lisbon and Porto to the stunning beaches of the Algarve and the ancient villages of the Douro Valley, Portugal has something for everyone.

In this travel guide, we will explore the best places to visit, the hidden gems that many tourists miss, and the best ways to connect with the local culture. We will also provide practical information on transportation, accommodations, and activities, as well as tips on how to avoid common mistakes and save time and money while traveling in Portugal.

Portugal is one of the oldest nations in Europe, with a history that dates back to the prehistoric era. The country was once a powerful maritime empire that spanned the globe, from Brazil to Goa, India. Portugal has also been influenced by many cultures throughout its history, including the Moors, Romans, and Celts.

Portuguese culture is a fusion of traditional and modern influences, with a strong emphasis on family, food, and faith. The country's art and architecture are characterized by intricate details and vibrant colors, with examples ranging from the medieval castles of Sintra to the contemporary buildings of Lisbon's Nations Park. Certainly! Portugal is a beautiful country with a rich history, vibrant culture, delicious food, and stunning landscapes. Here is a detailed Portugal travel guide:

- Best time to visit: The best time to visit Portugal is during the spring (March to May) and fall (September to November) when the weather is mild and the crowds are thinner. Summer (June to August) can be hot and crowded, but it is the best time to enjoy the beaches.
- Getting there: Portugal is easily accessible by air, with many major airlines flying to Lisbon, Porto, and Faro. There are also trains and buses available from Portugal and other European countries.
- Currency: The currency used in Portugal is the Euro.
- Language: The official language of Portugal is Portuguese, but English is widely spoken, especially in tourist areas.
- Accommodation: Portugal has a wide range of accommodation options, including hotels, hostels, guesthouses, and apartments. Prices vary depending on the location and season, but there are options to suit all budgets.

- Transportation: Portugal has an efficient transportation system, including buses, trains, and a metro system in Lisbon and Porto. Taxis are also widely available, but it is recommended to use licensed taxis with a meter.
- Food and drink: Portugal is known for its delicious cuisine, including seafood, meat, and pastries. Popular dishes include bacalhau (salted cod), cozido (meat stew), and pastéis de nata (custard tarts). Wine is also a major part of Portuguese culture, with many excellent varieties available.
- Sightseeing: Portugal has many beautiful sights to see, including historic cities, stunning beaches, and picturesque countryside. Some of the most popular destinations include Lisbon, Porto, Sintra, the Algarve region, and the Douro Valley.
- Culture and customs: Portugal has a rich cultural heritage, including traditional music, dance, and art. The people are friendly and welcoming, and it is customary to greet people with a handshake or kiss on the cheek.
- Safety: Portugal is a safe country to visit, but it is still important to take precautions against theft and pickpocketing, especially in crowded areas.

Overall, Portugal is a wonderful country to visit with something for everyone. Whether you are interested in history, culture, food, or natural beauty, there is plenty to see and do in this beautiful country.

Chapter 1.
The history

Portugal is one of the oldest nations in Europe, with a history that dates back to the prehistoric era. The country was once a powerful maritime empire that spanned the globe, from Brazil to Goa, India. Portugal has also been influenced by many cultures throughout its history, including the Moors, Romans, and Celts.

Portuguese culture is a fusion of traditional and modern influences, with a strong emphasis on family, food, and faith. The country's art and architecture are characterized by intricate details and vibrant colors, with examples ranging from the medieval castles of Sintra to the contemporary buildings of Lisbon's Nations Park.

In the 12th century, Portugal emerged as an independent kingdom when King Afonso Henriques defeated the Moors in the Battle of Ourique in 1139. He declared himself the first king of Portugal and established the House of Burgundy as the ruling dynasty. During the 15th and 16th centuries, Portugal became a major European power, with a vast overseas empire that included territories in Africa, Asia, and the Americas. This period is known as the Age of Discovery.

In 1498, Portuguese explorer Vasco da Gama discovered a sea route to India, establishing Portugal's dominance in the spice trade. In 1500, Pedro Álvares Cabral discovered Brazil, which would become the largest colony in the Portuguese Empire. Portugal's wealth and power continued to grow, but its monarchy was overthrown in 1910, following years of political instability and economic decline.

The Republic of Portugal was established, and the country faced a number of challenges in the 20th century, including two World Wars, a dictatorship under António de Oliveira Salazar, and a revolution in 1974 that led to democracy. In the 1980s and 1990s, Portugal underwent significant economic and social changes, joining the European Union in 1986 and adopting the euro as its currency in 1999.

Today, Portugal is a democratic country with a diverse economy that includes industries such as tourism, agriculture, and technology. Its cultural heritage is rich and varied, with influences from its history as a maritime nation, its Catholic tradition, and its proximity to Portugal and other European countries. Portugal is also known for its wine, cuisine, and fado music, which has been designated as a UNESCO World Heritage cultural treasure.

To delve deeper into Portugal's history, let us explore some of its key events and periods in greater detail:

The Age of Discovery:

As mentioned earlier, Portugal emerged as a major maritime power during the 15th and 16th centuries, with a vast overseas empire that included Brazil, Angola, Mozambique, and parts of India, China, and Indonesia. Portugal's explorers and sailors, such as Vasco da Gama, Ferdinand Magellan, and Bartolomeu Dias, helped map and navigate new trade routes and establish trading posts and colonies. The wealth and resources acquired through these ventures allowed Portugal to establish itself as a major European power, influencing art, science, and culture during the Renaissance period.

The Portuguese Empire:

The Portuguese Empire reached its peak in the 16th century, with a vast network of trading posts and colonies across Africa, Asia, and the Americas. However, the empire began to decline in the 17th century, due to competition from other European powers, economic challenges, and political instability at home. By the end of the 19th century, Portugal had lost most of its overseas territories, except for Angola, Mozambique, and some islands in the Atlantic.

The Estado Novo:

In 1932, António de Oliveira Salazar became prime minister of Portugal and established a dictatorship that lasted until 1974. The regime, known as the Estado Novo or New State, was characterized by authoritarianism, censorship, and a focus on economic development and stability. While the regime succeeded in modernizing Portugal's infrastructure and industry, it also suppressed dissent and violated human rights. The Estado Novo ended with the Carnation Revolution in 1974, a peaceful coup that brought democracy and freedom to Portugal.

Recent Developments:

Since the end of the dictatorship, Portugal has undergone significant economic and social changes. It joined the European Union in 1986, which brought about economic growth and investment. The country has also made significant progress in areas such as education, healthcare, and social welfare. However, Portugal has faced challenges in recent years, including economic crises, political corruption scandals, and demographic changes such as an aging population and declining birth rates.

In conclusion, Portugal's history is rich and complex, shaped by its geography, culture, and interactions with other peoples and nations. Despite facing challenges and setbacks over the centuries, Portugal has emerged as a vibrant and dynamic country, known for its beautiful landscapes, rich cultural heritage, and friendly people.

Cultural heritage, art and architecture

Portugal has a rich cultural heritage that dates back thousands of years, and its art and architecture reflect the country's long and diverse history. From prehistoric cave paintings to Roman ruins to medieval castles and Baroque palaces, Portugal is a treasure trove of artistic and architectural marvels. Here are some of the most notable examples:

- Prehistoric art: Portugal has some of the oldest cave paintings in Europe, dating back to the Upper Paleolithic period (around 20,000 BCE). The most famous example is the cave of Escoural, near Évora, which contains dozens of colorful depictions of animals and humans.

- Roman ruins: Portugal was part of the Roman Empire from the 2nd century BCE until the 5th century CE, and many Roman ruins can still be seen throughout the country. The most impressive are the Roman Temple of Évora, a well-preserved Corinthian-style temple from the 1st century CE, and the Conímbriga Archaeological Site, an extensive complex of Roman ruins near Coimbra.
- Gothic architecture: Portugal's Gothic period, which lasted from the 12th to the 16th centuries, left a lasting mark on the country's architecture. The most famous example is the Monastery of Batalha, a UNESCO World Heritage site that took over a century to build and features intricate Gothic details.
- Manueline style: The Manueline style emerged in the early 16th century during the reign of King Manuel I and is characterized by elaborate decorations featuring maritime motifs, such as ropes, anchors, and sea creatures. The most famous example of Manueline architecture is the Jerónimos Monastery in Lisbon, a stunning example of the style's intricate stonework.
- Baroque architecture: Portugal's Baroque period, which lasted from the late 17th to the mid-18th century, was marked by a flamboyant style featuring dramatic curves, ornate decorations, and bold colors. The most famous examples of Baroque architecture in Portugal are the Palácio Nacional de Mafra, a massive palace and monastery complex near Lisbon, and the Church of São Francisco in Porto, which features a gilded Baroque interior.

- Tiles: Portugal is famous for its ornate azulejos, or decorative tiles, which can be seen on buildings throughout the country. The tiles are often used to create intricate patterns and scenes, and can be found on everything from churches to train stations.
- Fado music: Fado is a form of traditional Portuguese music that originated in Lisbon in the early 19th century. The music is characterized by mournful melodies and lyrics that often deal with themes of love, loss, and longing. Fado can be heard in many Lisbon bars and restaurants, and there are also several fado museums and cultural centers throughout the city.
- Portuguese tiles: The use of tiles, or azulejos, is a defining feature of Portuguese architecture and decoration. The tiles were introduced in the 15th century and became particularly popular during the Baroque period. The tiles were used to decorate the facades of buildings, churches, and palaces, as well as the interiors of homes and public buildings. Many of the tiles depict scenes from Portugal's history and culture, such as the famous blue-and-white tiles at the São Bento railway station in Porto that depict scenes from the country's history.
- Renaissance architecture: Portugal's Renaissance period, which took place during the 16th century, saw a revival of classical styles and motifs. The most famous example of Renaissance architecture in Portugal is the Palace of Sintra, a former royal residence that features elegant facades and ornate interiors.
- Baroque sculpture: In addition to its ornate architecture, Portugal also has a rich tradition

of Baroque sculpture. The most famous example is the works of sculptor Joaquim Machado de Castro, whose masterpiece is the monumental equestrian statue of King John VI that stands in the Praça do Comércio in Lisbon.

- Traditional crafts: Portugal has a rich tradition of handicrafts, including ceramics, embroidery, weaving, and lace making. Many of these crafts have been passed down through generations and are still practiced today, particularly in the rural areas of the country. The town of Viana do Castelo, for example, is known for its intricate filigree jewelry, while the village of Manteigas is famous for its woolen blankets and shawls.

- Contemporary art: Portugal has a thriving contemporary art scene, with numerous galleries and museums showcasing the work of both Portuguese and international artists. The most famous contemporary art museum in Portugal is the Museu de Arte Contemporânea de Serralves in Porto, which features a diverse collection of modern and contemporary art in a striking minimalist building.

In summary, Portugal's cultural heritage, art, and architecture are diverse and multifaceted, reflecting the country's long and complex history. From prehistoric cave paintings to contemporary art installations, Portugal offers visitors a wealth of cultural treasures to discover and explore.

Chapter 2.
The main attractions in Portugal

Lisbon:

The capital city of Portugal is a vibrant and colorful destination with a rich history and culture. Highlights include the Belem Tower, Jeronimos Monastery, Sao Jorge Castle, and the Alfama neighborhood. Known for its rich history, stunning architecture, lively culture, and breathtaking vistas, Lisbon offers a unique blend of old-world charm and modern sophistication. Let's explore the various attractions that make Lisbon such a captivating place to visit:

- Historic Neighborhoods: Lisbon is famous for its picturesque and charming neighborhoods, each with its own distinct character. Alfama, the oldest district, is a maze of narrow streets, colorful houses, and Fado music. The Baixa district showcases grand squares, elegant buildings, and pedestrian-friendly streets, while Bairro Alto is renowned for its lively nightlife and trendy bars.

- Stunning Architecture: Lisbon boasts a diverse architectural heritage. The city is home to magnificent landmarks such as the Belém Tower, a UNESCO World Heritage site; the Jerónimos Monastery, an impressive example of Manueline architecture; and the São Jorge Castle, offering panoramic views of the city. The iconic 25 de Abril Bridge, reminiscent of the Golden Gate Bridge in San Francisco, adds to the city's allure.

- Fado Music: Fado is the soulful and melancholic traditional music of Portugal, and Lisbon is its birthplace. The Alfama district is particularly known for its Fado houses, where locals and tourists gather to experience the heartfelt performances. The emotionally charged lyrics and haunting melodies of Fado create a unique atmosphere that resonates with visitors.

- Culinary Delights: Lisbon is a food lover's paradise, offering a diverse array of culinary delights. From pastéis de nata (traditional custard tarts) to fresh seafood and delicious bacalhau (salted codfish) dishes, the city's gastronomy is sure to tantalize your taste buds. Don't miss visiting the vibrant Mercado da Ribeira, a food hall where you can sample a wide range of Portuguese cuisine.

- Vibrant Street Life: Lisbon's streets are vibrant and full of energy. From the bustling squares like Rossio and Praça do Comércio to the lively markets and local cafes, there's always something happening. The city's iconic yellow trams add a charming touch to the streetscape, and the famous Elevador de Santa Justa offers a unique way to reach the hilly neighborhoods.

- Cultural Offerings: Lisbon is a cultural hub with numerous museums, art galleries, and theaters. The Museu Nacional do Azulejo showcases the country's beautiful tile art, while the Museu Nacional de Arte Antiga houses an extensive collection of Portuguese and European art. The Centro Cultural de Belém hosts exhibitions, performances, and concerts, and the annual Lisbon Book Fair attracts book enthusiasts from far and wide.

- River Tagus and Coastline: Lisbon's location along the banks of the River Tagus (Rio Tejo) and its proximity to the Atlantic Ocean provide ample opportunities for enjoying water-related activities. Take a leisurely cruise along the river, relax on the nearby beaches of Cascais and Estoril, or venture out for surfing or sailing adventures.

- Day Trips: Lisbon serves as an excellent base for exploring the surrounding areas. You can take day trips to the fairytale-like village of Sintra, with its palaces and enchanting forests, or visit the charming town of Cascais. Additionally, the nearby town of Belém offers historical sites, including the Belém Tower and the stunning Jerónimos Monastery.

The opening and closing times of establishments in Lisbon, such as shops, restaurants, and attractions, may vary depending on the specific day of the week and the type of establishment. However, here are some general guidelines:

Shops:

Most shops in Lisbon are typically open from Monday to Saturday.

Opening hours vary, but a common schedule is from around 9:00 or 10:00 in the morning until 7:00 or 8:00 in the evening.

Some larger shopping malls and department stores may have extended hours, staying open until 10:00 or 11:00 at night.

Restaurants:

Lunchtime in Lisbon usually starts around 12:00 or 12:30 p.m. and continues until around 3:00 or 3:30 p.m.

Dinner service usually begins at around 7:00 or 7:30 p.m. and can continue until 10:00 or 11:00 p.m.

It's worth noting that dining times in Portugal tend to be a bit later compared to some other European countries.

Attractions and Museums:

The opening hours of attractions and museums in Lisbon can vary depending on the specific place.

Many attractions are typically open from around 10:00 a.m. to 6:00 p.m.

Some major attractions may have extended hours during the peak tourist season, staying open until 8:00 or 9:00 p.m.

It's important to check the official websites or contact the specific establishments you plan to visit in advance to confirm their opening and closing times, as there may be exceptions, seasonal variations, or special events that can affect their schedules.

Porto:

Located in the north of Portugal, Porto is famous for its historic center, Port wine cellars, and beautiful Douro River. Don't miss the Ribeira district, the Clerigos Tower, and the Sao Bento train station. It is the country's second-largest city after Lisbon and is known for its rich history, stunning architecture, port wine production, and lively atmosphere. Here are some key highlights and attractions of Porto:

- Historic City Center (Ribeira): The historic center of Porto, known as Ribeira, is a UNESCO World Heritage site. Its narrow winding streets, colorful buildings, and medieval architecture create a charming and picturesque atmosphere. You can explore the iconic Ribeira Square, visit the Porto Cathedral (Sé do Porto), and enjoy stunning views of the Douro River.
- Dom Luís I Bridge: This double-deck iron bridge is one of Porto's most iconic landmarks. Spanning the Douro River, it offers

breathtaking panoramic views of the city and the picturesque Vila Nova de Gaia district. You can walk across the upper level or take a tram ride to experience the beauty of the bridge.

- Port Wine Cellars: Porto is renowned for its production of port wine, and the city offers opportunities to visit the historic wine cellars in Vila Nova de Gaia, located just across the river from Porto. You can take tours of the cellars, learn about the wine-making process, and indulge in tastings of the famous port wine.
- Livraria Lello: Considered one of the most beautiful bookstores in the world, Livraria Lello is a must-visit attraction for book lovers and architecture enthusiasts. Its stunning neo-Gothic façade, intricate interior design, and impressive staircase make it a truly unique and enchanting place.
- Clerigos Tower: The Clérigos Tower is an iconic symbol of Porto's skyline. Climb the 240-step spiral staircase to reach the top and enjoy panoramic views of the city. The tower is part of the Clérigos Church and its Baroque architecture is worth exploring as well.
- Casa da Música: Porto is a hub of arts and culture, and Casa da Música is a modern architectural masterpiece that stands out. This concert hall hosts a variety of performances, including classical, contemporary, and jazz music. Even if you don't attend a concert, the building itself is worth admiring.
- São Bento Train Station: Known for its stunning azulejo (Portuguese ceramic tile) panels, São Bento Train Station is a beautiful architectural gem. The intricate blue and

white tiles depict historical events and scenes from Portuguese culture, creating a unique visual experience.

- Foz do Douro: Foz do Douro is a coastal district where the Douro River meets the Atlantic Ocean. It offers beautiful beaches, scenic promenades, and upscale restaurants. It's a great place to relax, take a walk along the waterfront, and enjoy breathtaking sunsets.

These are just a few highlights of what Porto has to offer. The city's lively atmosphere, friendly locals, and the fusion of tradition and modernity make it a captivating destination for visitors.

Algarve Beaches:

The Algarve region is home to some of the most beautiful beaches in Europe, with crystal-clear waters and sandy coves.

The Algarve region in southern Portugal is renowned for its stunning coastline and beautiful beaches. With its golden sands, crystal-clear waters, and dramatic cliffs, the Algarve offers a variety of beach experiences for every preference.

To obtain the most accurate and up-to-date information about the opening and closing times for Portugal beaches, as well as any potential closures or adjustments during holidays, I recommend reaching out to the local tourism board, the beach management authorities, or a nearby visitor center. They will be able to provide you with specific details tailored to your visit.

Here are some of the top beaches in the Algarve:

- Praia da Marinha: Considered one of the most beautiful beaches in Europe, Praia da Marinha is known for its impressive cliffs, rock formations, and clear turquoise waters. It's an ideal spot for snorkeling, exploring caves, and enjoying the natural beauty of the area.

The opening and closing times of Praia da Marinha may vary depending on the time of year and local regulations. During the summer season, which typically spans from June to September, most beaches in Portugal have longer opening hours to accommodate the influx of visitors. They generally open early in the morning, around 8 or 9 a.m., and close in the evening, between 6 and 8 p.m.

It's important to note that beach opening and closing times can be subject to change based on factors such as weather conditions, tides, and local regulations. Additionally, during certain periods, especially outside of the peak summer season, the beach may have reduced services or limited access. It is always advisable to check for updated information before planning your visit.

- Praia da Falésia: Located near the popular resort town of Albufeira, Praia da Falésia is a long stretch of golden sand backed by stunning red cliffs. This beach offers plenty of space to relax, walk along the shore, and enjoy the panoramic views.

The opening and closing times of Praia da Falésia may vary depending on the time of year and local regulations. During the summer season, which typically spans from June to September, beaches in Portugal tend to have longer opening hours to cater to the higher number of visitors. They generally open early in the morning, around 8 or 9 a.m., and close in the evening, between 6 and 8 p.m.

Regarding holidays and public holidays, beaches in Portugal are typically open during these times, although there may be adjustments to certain services or facilities. Public holidays in Portugal include New Year's Day (January 1), Easter Sunday (varies each year), Freedom Day (April 25), Labor Day (May 1), Portugal Day (June 10), and Christmas Day (December 25), among others.

- Praia de Dona Ana: Situated close to the city of Lagos, Praia de Dona Ana is often regarded as one of Lagos' most picturesque beaches. It features striking rock formations, small coves, and clear waters. The beach is easily accessible and has facilities such as restaurants and restrooms nearby.
- Praia do Camilo: Another gem near Lagos, Praia do Camilo is accessed via a steep staircase, but the effort is worth it. The beach is nestled between cliffs, offering a secluded and intimate atmosphere. It boasts rock arches, sea caves, and inviting turquoise waters.

- Praia de Benagil: Located near the village of Benagil, this beach is famous for its mesmerizing sea cave known as the Benagil Cave or Algar de Benagil. You can reach the cave by boat or kayak and admire its natural beauty. The beach itself is small but charming, with golden sands and clear waters.
- Praia de Faro: Situated on the barrier island of Ilha de Faro, Praia de Faro is easily accessible from the city of Faro. This expansive beach offers a mix of bustling areas with beach bars and restaurants, as well as quieter sections for relaxation. It's a popular choice for families and offers a range of water sports activities.
- Praia da Rocha: Located near the city of Portimão, Praia da Rocha is a lively and vibrant beach known for its extensive sandy shore and impressive rock formations. It offers a vibrant atmosphere with beach bars, restaurants, and water sports options.
- Praia de Odeceixe: Situated on the western coast of the Algarve, Praia de Odeceixe is a picturesque beach surrounded by rugged cliffs and the Odeceixe River. It's a great spot for surfers, nature lovers, and those seeking a more tranquil and unspoiled beach experience.

These are just a few examples of the many beautiful beaches in the Algarve. Whether you're looking for scenic beauty, water sports, family-friendly areas, or secluded coves, the Algarve offers a wide range of beach options to suit every preference.

Sintra

Sintra is a charming town located in the foothills of the Sintra Mountains, just a short distance from Lisbon, Portugal. Known for its fairytale-like atmosphere, lush landscapes, and impressive architectural heritage, Sintra is a UNESCO World Heritage site and a popular destination for visitors. Here are some of the main attractions and highlights of Sintra:

- Pena Palace: One of the most iconic landmarks in Sintra, Pena Palace is a colorful and whimsical palace perched atop a hill. Its eclectic architectural style combines elements of Romanticism, Moorish, and Manueline styles. The palace is surrounded by lush gardens and offers panoramic views of the surrounding area.
- Quinta da Regaleira: This mystical and enchanting estate is a must-visit in Sintra. It features a Neo-Manueline mansion, lush gardens, underground tunnels, and hidden

symbolism. The highlight is the Initiation Well, a mesmerizing underground spiral staircase with intricate symbolism.

- Moorish Castle: The ruins of the Moorish Castle date back to the 9th century and offer a glimpse into the region's history. Visitors can explore the castle walls, towers, and enjoy sweeping views of the town and surrounding countryside.

- National Palace of Sintra: Located in the heart of the town, the National Palace of Sintra is a well-preserved medieval palace. It is known for its distinctive conical chimneys and stunning tile work. The palace showcases a mix of architectural styles, including Moorish, Gothic, and Manueline.

- Monserrate Palace: Situated in a lush park, Monserrate Palace is a captivating blend of Gothic, Indian, and Moorish architectural styles. The palace features intricate details, beautiful gardens, and exotic plants from around the world.

- Sintra-Cascais Natural Park: The Sintra-Cascais Natural Park surrounds the town of Sintra and offers breathtaking natural landscapes. It encompasses lush forests, rugged cliffs, and picturesque coastal areas. There are numerous hiking trails, including the popular trail to Cabo da Roca, the westernmost point of mainland Europe.

- Sintra's Historical Center: The town of Sintra itself is a delightful place to explore. Its historical center is filled with narrow cobblestone streets, traditional shops, and charming cafes. Strolling through the town, you can soak in its romantic atmosphere and admire the beautiful architecture.

- Sintra Tram: Taking a ride on the Sintra Tram is a unique experience. This vintage tram connects Sintra to Praia das Maçãs, a nearby beach. The tram ride offers scenic views of the countryside as it winds its way through the hills.

Sintra's unique blend of natural beauty, historical landmarks, and enchanting ambiance make it a captivating destination. Its proximity to Lisbon makes it easily accessible, and a day trip from the capital is a popular choice for many visitors.

Peneda-Geres Park

Peneda-Gerês National Park, also known as Parque Nacional da Peneda-Gerês, is a stunning natural reserve located in the northwestern part of Portugal. Established in 1971, it is the only national park in Portugal and covers an area of approximately 700 square kilometers. Peneda-Gerês is known for its exceptional biodiversity, breathtaking landscapes, and rich cultural heritage. Here are some key features and attractions of the park:

- Scenic Landscapes: Peneda-Gerês National Park offers diverse and awe-inspiring landscapes. You'll find rugged mountains, deep valleys, pristine rivers and streams, waterfalls, and dense forests. The park's highest peak is Mount Peneda, reaching an elevation of 1,416 meters, offering stunning panoramic views.
- Flora and Fauna: The park is home to a remarkable array of plant and animal species. Its diverse ecosystem includes oak and pine forests, heathlands, and meadows. You may encounter wildlife such as wild horses (Garrano horses), deer, wolves, boars, otters, and various bird species, including golden eagles and black storks.
- Hiking and Nature Trails: Peneda-Gerês is a paradise for outdoor enthusiasts, offering a network of well-maintained trails for hiking and exploring. The park provides a wide range of hiking routes, from leisurely walks to more challenging treks. Popular trails include the Seven Lagoons (Sete Lagoas) trail and the Soajo Megalithic Route.
- Waterfalls and Natural Pools: The park features several beautiful waterfalls and natural pools, perfect for cooling off during the warmer months. The Tahiti Waterfall, Arado Waterfall, and Portela do Homem Waterfall are among the most renowned. Some locations, such as the Poço Azul, offer tranquil pools for swimming.

- Traditional Villages and Cultural Heritage: Peneda-Gerês is dotted with charming traditional villages that provide insights into the local culture and heritage. Soajo, Lindoso, and Castro Laboreiro are notable examples, showcasing traditional granite houses, granaries (espigueiros), and historical landmarks. The park is also home to ancient ruins, including Roman roads and prehistoric rock carvings.
- Outdoor Activities: The park offers a wide range of outdoor activities for visitors to enjoy. These include birdwatching, fishing, canoeing or kayaking in the park's rivers and reservoirs, mountain biking, and horseback riding. Camping is also permitted in designated areas, allowing visitors to immerse themselves in the natural surroundings.
- Thermal Spas: Peneda-Gerês has several thermal spas where you can relax and rejuvenate in mineral-rich waters. The spas, such as Caldas do Gerês and Pedra Bela, offer a range of wellness treatments and therapies.
- Cultural Events and Festivals: Throughout the year, Peneda-Gerês hosts cultural events and traditional festivals that celebrate the local customs, music, dance, and gastronomy. These events provide an opportunity to experience the vibrant local culture and interact with the community.

National parks in Portugal typically have year-round access, but certain facilities and services within the park may have varying schedules. The park's opening and closing times are generally determined by daylight hours, allowing visitors to enjoy the natural beauty during daylight. During the summer months, when the days are longer, the park may have extended opening hours.

Peneda-Gerês National Park offers a remarkable blend of natural beauty, biodiversity, and cultural heritage. Whether you're seeking outdoor adventures, peaceful nature walks, or a glimpse into the region's history, this park provides an unforgettable experience for nature lovers and explorers.

Coimbra

Coimbra is a historic city located in central Portugal, about halfway between Lisbon and Porto. It is best known for its prestigious university, Coimbra University, which is one of the oldest universities in Europe and a UNESCO World Heritage site. Here are some key highlights and attractions of Coimbra:

- Coimbra University: The University of Coimbra is a major attraction and a symbol of the city. Founded in 1290, it features stunning architecture, including the Joanine Library with its intricate baroque design and the beautiful University Tower. The academic traditions and historic atmosphere make it a must-visit.

- Coimbra Old Town: The historic center of Coimbra is a charming area to explore. It is characterized by narrow streets, medieval buildings, and picturesque squares. Visit the Sé Velha (Old Cathedral), a Romanesque masterpiece, and enjoy the lively atmosphere of Praça do Comércio.

- Monastery of Santa Clara-a-Velha: This medieval monastery is an architectural gem situated near the Mondego River. It offers a fascinating glimpse into the city's history and features well-preserved ruins, beautiful cloisters, and an informative visitor center.

- Monastery of Santa Cruz: Located in the city center, the Monastery of Santa Cruz is one of Coimbra's most important religious sites. It houses the tombs of the first two kings of Portugal and exhibits remarkable Gothic and Manueline architectural styles.

- Botanical Garden of the University of Coimbra: This serene and peaceful garden is one of the oldest in Portugal. It features a vast collection of plants, including rare species, and offers a tranquil setting for a leisurely stroll or a picnic.

- Portugal dos Pequenitos: This miniature park is a popular attraction, especially for families. It showcases scaled-down replicas of Portuguese houses, monuments, and cultural landmarks, allowing visitors to explore Portugal in a miniaturized form.

- Fado Music: Coimbra is also known as one of the centers of Fado music in Portugal. Fado de Coimbra is a unique style of Fado associated with the city, typically performed by male students. Many local restaurants and bars offer Fado performances, providing an opportunity to immerse yourself in this captivating musical tradition.

- Traditional Cuisine: Coimbra offers a delightful culinary scene, showcasing traditional Portuguese cuisine. Don't miss the chance to taste local specialties such as Chanfana (roasted goat or lamb), Leitão (suckling pig), and Queijo da Serra (Serra da Estrela cheese).

Fatima Shrine

The Fatima Shrine, officially known as the Sanctuary of Our Lady of Fatima, is one of the most important Catholic pilgrimage sites in the world. Located in the small town of Fatima in central Portugal, the shrine attracts millions of visitors each year who come to pay homage to the Virgin Mary and commemorate the reported apparitions of the Virgin Mary to three young shepherd children in 1917. Here are some key features and attractions of the Fatima Shrine:

- Basilica of Our Lady of the Rosary: The centerpiece of the Fatima Shrine is the Basilica of Our Lady of the Rosary. This grand neo-classical church was built in 1928 and houses the tombs of the three shepherd children: Saint Francisco Marto, Saint Jacinta Marto, and Sister Lucia dos Santos. The basilica's interior is adorned with beautiful stained glass windows depicting the mysteries of the rosary.
- Chapel of Apparitions: The Chapel of Apparitions is located in the exact spot where the Virgin Mary is said to have appeared to the shepherd children. The chapel marks the heart of the shrine and features a statue of Our Lady of Fatima. Pilgrims gather here to pray, leave offerings, and light candles as a sign of devotion.
- Way of the Cross: The Fatima Shrine has a Way of the Cross, also known as the Via Sacra or Sacred Way. It consists of 14 stations that depict the path Jesus took on his way to Calvary. Pilgrims can follow this path, meditating on each station and reflecting on the Passion of Christ.
- Basilica of the Holy Trinity: Inaugurated in 2007, the Basilica of the Holy Trinity is one of the largest Catholic churches in the world. It was built to accommodate the increasing number of pilgrims visiting the shrine. The basilica's modern design features a circular shape, and it can hold up to 9,000 people.

- Aljustrel: Aljustrel is the small village near Fatima where the shepherd children lived. Pilgrims can visit the homes of Lucia, Francisco, and Jacinta, which have been preserved as a museum. The museum displays personal items and provides insights into the lives of the children and their encounters with the Virgin Mary.
- Candlelight Processions: A notable tradition at the Fatima Shrine is the candlelight processions that take place in the evenings. Pilgrims gather holding candles, and as darkness falls, they proceed to the Chapel of Apparitions, reciting prayers and singing hymns. The sight of thousands of candles illuminating the night creates a deeply moving and spiritual atmosphere.
- Pilgrimage Events: The Fatima Shrine hosts several significant events throughout the year, attracting pilgrims from all over the world. Notably, May 13th and October 13th mark the anniversaries of the apparitions and draw massive crowds. On these occasions, special Masses, processions, and celebrations take place.

Obidos

Óbidos is a picturesque medieval town located in the Centro Region of Portugal, about 85 kilometers north of Lisbon. Enclosed within well-preserved walls, Óbidos is known for its narrow cobbled streets, charming houses adorned with bougainvillea, and a rich historical and cultural heritage. Here are some of the highlights and attractions of Óbidos:

- Castle of Óbidos: Dominating the town's skyline, the Castle of Óbidos is a medieval fortress that dates back to the 12th century. With its imposing walls and towers, it offers panoramic views of the town and surrounding countryside. Today, the castle houses a luxurious hotel, allowing visitors to experience a stay within its historic walls.
- Óbidos Town Walls: The town is entirely enclosed by well-preserved medieval walls, which you can walk along for a unique perspective of Óbidos. The walls provide picturesque views of the town's white houses, red-roofed buildings, and the surrounding countryside.
- Santa Maria Church: Located in the main square of Óbidos, the Church of Santa Maria is a beautiful example of Portuguese Gothic architecture. The church features intricate stained glass windows and an impressive interior with decorative tiles and religious artworks.
- Rua Direita: Rua Direita, or the main street of Óbidos, is a charming pedestrian thoroughfare lined with shops, cafes, and artisanal stores. Walking along this street, you can admire the traditional architecture, browse for souvenirs,

taste local treats like Ginjinha (a cherry liqueur), and soak in the vibrant atmosphere.

- Capela de São Martinho: The Chapel of São Martinho is a small but significant religious site in Óbidos. It is believed to be the place where the marriage of King Afonso V and his cousin, Princess Isabel, took place in the 15th century. The chapel features beautiful tilework and an intricately carved altarpiece.
- Festival of Óbidos: Throughout the year, Óbidos hosts various festivals and events that attract visitors from far and wide. The most famous event is the Óbidos Christmas Village, where the town is transformed into a magical winter wonderland with lights, decorations, and a Christmas market.
- Chocolate Festival: Óbidos is also renowned for its annual Chocolate Festival, held in the spring. During the festival, the town becomes a paradise for chocolate lovers, with chocolate sculptures, tastings, workshops, and a wide array of chocolate-related products.
- Literary History: Óbidos has a literary heritage, as it was declared a Literary Village in 2015. The town hosts literary events, book fairs, and has a bookstore dedicated to promoting Portuguese literature.

Óbidos is a place where time seems to have stood still, offering visitors a glimpse into Portugal's medieval past. Its well-preserved architecture, vibrant festivals, and rich cultural scene make it a delightful destination for history enthusiasts, art lovers, and those seeking a unique and enchanting experience.

Douro River

The Douro River is indeed a captivating tourist attraction in Portugal, renowned for its breathtaking landscapes, historic vineyards, and charming riverside towns. Let's delve into the reasons why the Douro River holds such allure for visitors.

- Scenic Beauty: The Douro River is renowned for its stunning natural beauty. As it winds through Portugal's terraced vineyards and rolling hills, the river offers awe-inspiring vistas at every turn. The steep slopes covered in vineyards create a unique and picturesque landscape that has been designated as a UNESCO World Heritage site.
- Wine Region: The Douro Valley is one of the oldest and most celebrated wine regions in the world. Famous for its production of port wine, the region is dotted with centuries-old vineyards and wineries. Visitors can explore the vineyards, learn about the winemaking process, and sample a variety of exquisite wines. Wine tours and tastings are popular

activities that allow tourists to immerse themselves in the rich viticultural heritage of the area.

- River Cruises: Cruising along the Douro River is an exceptional way to experience the region. Numerous river cruise operators offer journeys that take passengers along the river, passing through the breathtaking landscapes and stopping at charming towns and villages along the way. These cruises provide a leisurely and luxurious way to enjoy the Douro Valley's beauty while indulging in local cuisine and wines.

- Historic Towns and Villages: The Douro River is flanked by an array of quaint and historic towns and villages that exude charm and character. One such town is Pinhão, known for its beautiful tile-adorned train station and its role as a hub for port wine production. Other notable towns include Peso da Régua, which serves as a gateway to the Douro wine region, and Lamego, home to the impressive Nossa Senhora dos Remédios Sanctuary. These towns offer a glimpse into the region's rich history and provide opportunities to explore local traditions and architecture.

- Outdoor Activities: The Douro River region is a haven for outdoor enthusiasts. Travelers can engage in activities such as hiking, cycling, and boating, allowing them to immerse themselves in the region's natural beauty. The river's surroundings also offer fantastic opportunities for photography, with vineyard-covered hills, ancient terraces, and picturesque riverbanks.

- Gastronomy and Cuisine: The Douro Valley is a gastronomic delight, offering a delectable array of traditional Portuguese dishes. The region's cuisine emphasizes local ingredients, including fresh fish, olive oil, and almonds. Visitors can savor traditional dishes like bacalhau (salted codfish), roasted meats, and hearty stews. Coupled with the region's renowned wines, the Douro Valley provides a memorable culinary experience.

Overall, the Douro River captivates tourists with its natural beauty, historic charm, world-class wines, and delicious cuisine. Whether exploring the vineyards, embarking on a river cruise, or simply savoring the breathtaking landscapes, visitors are sure to be enchanted by the Douro River's allure.

Lisbon Nations Park

Lisbon Nations Park is a modern waterfront district located in the eastern part of Lisbon, Portugal's capital city. It was originally developed as the site of the Expo '98, a World Exposition held in Lisbon to commemorate the 500th anniversary of the arrival of

Vasco da Gama in India. After the event, the area was transformed into a vibrant and contemporary neighborhood that has become a major tourist attraction.

Here are some key features and attractions within Lisbon Nations Park:

- Waterfront Area: The park stretches along the Tagus River, offering a scenic waterfront promenade where visitors can enjoy stunning views of the river and the Vasco da Gama Bridge, one of Europe's longest bridges. The waterfront area is perfect for leisurely strolls, cycling, or simply relaxing while enjoying the picturesque surroundings.
- Oceanário de Lisboa (Lisbon Oceanarium): One of the standout attractions in Lisbon Nations Park is the Oceanário de Lisboa, which is one of the largest aquariums in Europe. It houses an impressive array of marine life from different habitats, including sharks, penguins, sea otters, and tropical fish. The Oceanarium offers educational exhibits and interactive displays, making it a fascinating experience for visitors of all ages.
- Pavilhão do Conhecimento (Knowledge Pavilion): The Knowledge Pavilion is a science museum focused on interactive exhibits that explore various scientific concepts and technologies. It offers hands-on experiences, workshops, and temporary exhibitions, making it a great place for learning and discovery.
- Cable Car: The park features a cable car system that provides visitors with an aerial view of the area. The cable car ride offers a unique

perspective of Lisbon Nations Park, allowing passengers to enjoy panoramic views of the river, the park, and the surrounding cityscape.

- Vasco da Gama Tower: Standing tall at 145 meters, the Vasco da Gama Tower is one of Lisbon's iconic landmarks. It offers a panoramic viewing platform that provides breathtaking views of the city and the Tagus River. The tower also houses a luxury hotel and a revolving restaurant, offering a memorable dining experience.
- Gardens and Public Spaces: Lisbon Nations Park features beautifully landscaped gardens, open spaces, and recreational areas where visitors can relax and enjoy nature. The park is dotted with sculptures, fountains, and public art installations, creating a pleasant atmosphere for leisure activities or picnics.
- Shopping and Entertainment: The Vasco da Gama Shopping Center is located within the park and offers a wide range of shops, boutiques, restaurants, and cinemas. It provides a convenient place for shopping, dining, and entertainment options.

Lisbon Nations Park is well-connected to the rest of the city by public transportation, including metro, bus, and train service Here are some common opening and closing times for popular attractions in Lisbon Nations Park:

Oceanário de Lisboa (Lisbon Oceanarium):

Opening hours: Usually opens around 10:00 AM.

Closing hours: Typically closes around 6:00 PM or 7:00 PM.

Pavilhão do Conhecimento (Knowledge Pavilion):

Opening hours: Generally opens around 10:00 AM.

Closing hours: Typically closes around 6:00 PM or 7:00 PM.

It is a vibrant district that combines modern architecture, cultural attractions, and leisure facilities. Whether you're interested in science, marine life, or simply enjoying the outdoors, Lisbon Nations Park offers a diverse range of experiences for visitors to enjoy.

Batalha Monastery

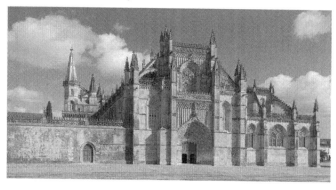

The Batalha Monastery, also known as the Monastery of Santa Maria da Vitória, is a magnificent Gothic-style monastery located in the town of Batalha, Portugal. It is recognized as a UNESCO World Heritage site and is renowned for its exceptional architectural beauty and historical significance.

The Batalha Monastery was built to commemorate the victory of the Portuguese forces over the Castilians at the Battle of Aljubarrota in 1385. Construction of the monastery began in 1386 and continued for over a century, resulting in a fusion of architectural styles, primarily Gothic and Manueline (Portuguese late Gothic). The intricate details, ornate decorations, and the sheer scale of the building make it a remarkable example of Portuguese Gothic architecture.

The monastery consists of several notable areas:

- Founder's Chapel (Capela do Fundador): This chapel is the burial site of the monastery's founder, King John I, and his wife, Queen Philippa of Lancaster. The chapel is adorned with beautiful stained glass windows and intricate stone carvings.
- Royal Cloister (Claustro Real): The Royal Cloister is a breathtaking architectural masterpiece, characterized by delicate tracery and intricate detailing. It is considered one of the most remarkable examples of Manueline style in Portugal.
- Unfinished Chapels: The monastery's construction was never fully completed, and this is particularly evident in the unfinished chapels. The absence of a roof provides a unique perspective on the building's intricate vaulting and reveals the skill of the craftsmen involved.
- Chapter House (Capítulo):

The Batalha Monastery is open to visitors, allowing them to explore its architectural wonders and learn about its historical significance. As for the opening and closing times, it's essential to note that these hours can vary, especially during holidays and special events. Therefore, it is advisable to check the official website or contact the monastery directly to obtain accurate and up-to-date information regarding its operating hours.

When planning a visit to the Batalha Monastery, it is recommended to allocate a few hours to fully appreciate the beauty of the site and explore its different sections. The monastery offers guided tours that provide valuable insights into its history and architectural features. Visitors can also take advantage of the visitor center, which provides additional information about the monastery and the Battle of Aljubarrota.

Ponte 25 de Abril

Ponte 25 de Abril, also known as the 25th of April Bridge, is an iconic suspension bridge that spans the Tagus River in Lisbon, Portugal. It is one of the most recognizable landmarks in the city and an important symbol of its history and progress.

The bridge was completed in 1966 and was originally named Ponte Salazar after the Portuguese dictator António de Oliveira Salazar. However, after the Carnation Revolution on April 25, 1974, which marked the end of the authoritarian regime and the beginning of democracy in Portugal, the bridge was renamed Ponte 25 de Abril to commemorate the event.

Here are some key features and facts about Ponte 25 de Abril:

- Design: The bridge's design is often compared to the Golden Gate Bridge in San Francisco, USA, as both were designed by the same company, the American Bridge Company. It has a total length of 2.3 kilometers (1.4 miles) and a central span of 1.2 kilometers (0.75 miles). The bridge's towers reach a height of 190 meters (623 feet).
- Transportation: Ponte 25 de Abril serves as a crucial transportation link, connecting the city of Lisbon to the municipalities of Almada and Costa da Caparica. It carries both road and rail traffic. The upper deck accommodates six lanes for vehicle traffic, while the lower deck carries a railway line that connects Lisbon to the southern part of the country.
- Views: The bridge offers spectacular views of Lisbon's skyline and the Tagus River. It is particularly breathtaking when viewed from popular viewpoints such as the Santa Catarina viewpoint or from across the river in Almada. Visitors can also enjoy the stunning panorama while cruising along the Tagus River on boat tours.
- Public Transportation: The bridge is accessible to pedestrians and cyclists through designated walkways and cycling paths. It is possible to cross the bridge on foot, providing a unique perspective and a memorable experience.

- Similarities to the Golden Gate Bridge: Ponte 25 de Abril bears a resemblance to the Golden Gate Bridge due to its red color and suspension design. However, it is worth noting that the bridge was originally painted green but was later repainted to its current red color.

Visitors to Lisbon often appreciate the grandeur and significance of Ponte 25 de Abril. Its imposing structure, historical importance, and the picturesque views it offers make it a popular attraction for both tourists and locals. Whether crossing the bridge, taking photos from various viewpoints, or simply admiring its architectural beauty, Ponte 25 de Abril stands as an emblem of Lisbon's history and a symbol of the city's connection between its past and future.

Seven Cities Park

Seven Cities Park, also known as Parque Natural da Lagoa das Sete Cidades, is a breathtaking natural park located on the island of São Miguel in the Azores archipelago, Portugal. It is renowned for its stunning landscape, including twin lakes, lush greenery, and picturesque vistas. Here's an overview of the Seven Cities Park and its key features:

- Lakes: The park is centered around the twin lakes of Lagoa Azul (Blue Lake) and Lagoa Verde (Green Lake). These lakes are set within a volcanic crater and are famous for their contrasting colors. The Blue Lake has a vibrant blue hue, while the Green Lake exhibits shades of green. The lakes provide a captivating backdrop and are a popular subject for photographers and nature lovers.
- Hiking Trails: Seven Cities Park offers a variety of hiking trails that allow visitors to explore the natural beauty of the area. The trails range from easy walks to more challenging hikes, offering different perspectives of the lakes and surrounding landscapes. Popular routes include the Miradouro da Vista do Rei, which provides a panoramic view of the lakes, and the Serra Devassa trail, which takes you through verdant hills and offers breathtaking vistas.
- Vista do Rei Viewpoint: The Vista do Rei viewpoint is one of the most famous viewpoints in the Azores. It offers a sweeping view of the twin lakes, surrounded by lush green hills and valleys. This viewpoint was historically a favored spot for Portuguese monarchs, who would come to admire the majestic scenery.
- Flora and Fauna: Seven Cities Park is home to a rich diversity of flora and fauna. The park's lush vegetation includes endemic and exotic species, with vibrant flowers and endemic Azorean laurel forests. Birdwatchers will

appreciate the variety of bird species that inhabit the area, including Azores bullfinches and buzzards.

- Picnicking and Recreation: The park provides several picnic areas where visitors can relax and enjoy the peaceful surroundings. It's an ideal spot for a picnic, surrounded by the beauty of nature. Additionally, the lakes offer opportunities for water-based activities like kayaking or canoeing.

- Cultural Heritage: The area surrounding Seven Cities Park is steeped in folklore and legends. According to local folklore, the twin lakes were formed by the tears of a princess and a shepherd who were forbidden from being together. The tale adds a touch of mystique to the natural beauty of the park.

Visiting Seven Cities Park allows travelers to immerse themselves in the natural splendor of the Azores. Its scenic lakes, hiking trails, and peaceful ambiance make it a paradise for nature enthusiasts and those seeking tranquility. Whether you're capturing the stunning views, exploring the trails, or simply enjoying a picnic, Seven Cities Park offers a memorable experience in the heart of São Miguel Island.

Mafra Palace

Mafra Palace, known as Palácio Nacional de Mafra in Portuguese, is an impressive Baroque palace and monastery located in Mafra, a town in the Lisbon District of Portugal. It is one of the most significant historical and cultural landmarks in the country. Here is an overview of Mafra Palace and its notable features:

- History: Construction of Mafra Palace began in 1717 and lasted for over 13 years, finally being completed in 1730. The palace was commissioned by King João V as a grand monument to fulfill a vow he made to build a monastery if his wife, Queen Maria Anna of Austria, gave him descendants. The palace was intended to house a Franciscan monastery, a royal palace, and a basilica.
- Architecture: Mafra Palace is a massive structure, covering an area of around four hectares. It is a prime example of Baroque architecture and reflects the opulence and grandeur of the time. The palace facade is adorned with intricate carvings and

49

sculptures, while the interior boasts impressive halls, chapels, and rooms embellished with beautiful artworks, ornate details, and luxurious materials.

- Basilica: The Basilica of Mafra Palace is a significant part of the complex. It is an enormous church with six organs, which are still in working condition, making it one of the largest collections of historical organs in the world. The basilica is known for its stunning marble flooring, gilded altarpieces, and magnificent pipe organs, creating an awe-inspiring religious setting.
- Library: Mafra Palace is also renowned for its library, the Biblioteca Joanina. The library houses an extensive collection of more than 36,000 ancient books, including works from the 14th to the 19th centuries. The books are preserved in ornate wooden bookshelves and are protected by resident bats who help to prevent book-damaging insects.
- Cloisters: The palace features two majestic cloisters, the Claustro Grande (Great Cloister) and the Claustro dos Capuchos (Cloister of the Capuchins). The Claustro Grande is a massive courtyard with ornate arcades, statues, and fountains. The Claustro dos Capuchos is a smaller, more tranquil cloister that was exclusively used by the monks.
- Ceremonial Hall: The Sala dos Atos (Ceremonial Hall) is a magnificent hall within the palace that was used for important ceremonies and events. It is adorned with intricate woodwork, painted ceilings, and splendid chandeliers, showcasing the opulence and grandeur of the palace.

Visiting Mafra Palace allows travelers to immerse themselves in the rich history and architectural beauty of Portugal. The palace offers guided tours that provide insights into the fascinating stories, cultural significance, and artistic treasures housed within its walls. It is a must-visit destination for history enthusiasts, architecture lovers, and anyone interested in experiencing the grandeur of Portugal's past.

Guimaraes Castle

Guimarães Castle, known as Castelo de Guimarães in Portuguese, is a medieval fortress located in the city of Guimarães, in the northern part of Portugal. It holds significant historical and cultural importance as it is considered the birthplace of Portugal and has been recognized as a UNESCO World Heritage site. Here's an overview of Guimarães Castle and its notable features:

- Historical Significance: Guimarães Castle played a crucial role in the foundation of the

Portuguese nation. It was here that Afonso Henriques, the first King of Portugal, was born in 1109. Afonso Henriques led the struggle for independence from the Kingdom of León, and it was under his reign that Portugal began to take shape as an independent country.

- Architecture: The castle is a fine example of medieval military architecture. It features sturdy stone walls, defensive towers, and a central keep. The original construction dates back to the 10th century, with subsequent modifications and additions over the centuries. The castle's strategic position atop a hill provides commanding views of the surrounding area.

- Keep and Towers: The central keep, known as the Torre de Menagem, is the tallest structure within the castle complex. It served as a fortified residence and a strategic stronghold. Visitors can climb to the top of the tower and enjoy panoramic views of Guimarães and its surroundings. Additionally, there are other defensive towers within the castle, each with its own unique features.

- Archaeological Museum: The castle houses the Guimarães Archaeological Museum, which exhibits artifacts related to the castle's history and the region's archaeology. The museum provides insights into the medieval period, showcasing objects such as armor, weapons, and pottery.

- Surrounding Area: The castle is located in the heart of Guimarães, a charming city known for its well-preserved medieval architecture. The historical center of Guimarães is also a UNESCO World Heritage site and offers visitors the chance to explore narrow streets, traditional houses, and picturesque squares.

- Cultural Events: Guimarães Castle is a venue for cultural events and festivities, including historical reenactments, medieval festivals, and concerts. These events bring the castle to life, providing visitors with a glimpse into the past and adding to the vibrant atmosphere of the site.

Visiting Guimarães Castle allows travelers to immerse themselves in Portuguese history and experience the birthplace of the nation. The castle's imposing architecture, historical significance, and the surrounding medieval city of Guimarães make it a popular destination for tourists interested in Portugal's rich heritage.

Chapter 3.
The "hidden gems" of Portugal

Monsanto Village:

Monsanto is a unique and picturesque village located in the Idanha-a-Nova municipality of Portugal. Often referred to as the "Most Portuguese Village in Portugal," Monsanto is known for its charming atmosphere, traditional architecture, and its integration with the natural surroundings. Here is an overview of Monsanto Village:

- Historical Significance: Monsanto has a rich history dating back to prehistoric times, and evidence of human settlement in the area can be traced back thousands of years. The village was a strategic stronghold during the Roman and Moorish periods due to its elevated location and natural defenses.

- Unique Architecture: What sets Monsanto apart is its integration with the granite boulders and rock formations that surround it. Houses are built into and around giant boulders, and even the streets and steps are made of stone. This organic integration with the natural environment creates a visually stunning and distinctive appearance.

- Castle of Monsanto: Perched on a hilltop, the Castle of Monsanto is a prominent landmark in the village. It dates back to the 12th century and offers panoramic views of the surrounding countryside. Visitors can explore the castle ruins and soak in the historical ambiance.

- Village Attractions: Wandering through Monsanto's narrow streets is like stepping back in time. The village has traditional houses, some with unique features such as doorways carved into rock formations. There are also several chapels, a pillory, and the Church of Saint Salvador, which features Gothic and Manueline architectural elements.

- Natural Beauty: Monsanto is situated in the midst of beautiful natural landscapes. The village is surrounded by vast forests, rolling hills, and impressive granite rock formations. This natural setting provides ample opportunities for outdoor activities such as hiking, birdwatching, and enjoying scenic walks.

- Opening and Closing Times: The village of Monsanto does not have specific opening and closing times as it is a residential area. Visitors can explore the village at their leisure, wandering through the streets, visiting the castle ruins, and enjoying the picturesque surroundings. However, it is advisable to respect the residents' privacy and local customs while exploring the village.

Monsanto Village offers a captivating blend of history, culture, and natural beauty. Its unique architecture, integration with the landscape, and tranquil ambiance make it a hidden gem in the Portuguese countryside. Whether you're a history enthusiast, nature lover, or simply seeking a charming and authentic experience, Monsanto is well worth a visit.

Piodao Village:

A charming village located in the Serra do Açor mountain range, known for its well-preserved slate houses with blue doors and windows, and the beautiful natural surroundings.

Piodão Village, located in the Arganil municipality of central Portugal, is a charming and well-preserved village known for its traditional slate houses and picturesque setting. As a residential village, Piodão does not have strict opening and closing times. However, certain establishments within the village, such as restaurants and cafes, may have their own operating hours. Here's an overview of Piodão Village:

- Historical Significance: Piodão is classified as one of Portugal's historical villages and is renowned for its architectural heritage. The village has maintained its traditional appearance with narrow streets, stone houses with slate roofs, and a unique layout that blends harmoniously with the surrounding landscape.

- Traditional Architecture: The houses in Piodão are made of schist, a type of slate stone, which gives the village a distinct appearance. The buildings have whitewashed walls and dark gray slate roofs, creating a beautiful contrast against the green hills and mountains that surround the village.

- Streets and Alleys: Piodão's layout consists of winding streets and alleys, often made of stone, which add to the village's charm. Strolling through the narrow passages allows visitors to appreciate the traditional architecture up close and explore the village at their own pace.

- Santa Maria Church: Piodão is home to the Santa Maria Church, a small but significant religious building in the village. The church features simple, whitewashed walls and a bell tower. It is a place of worship and a symbol of the community's faith.

- Natural Surroundings: Piodão is nestled in the Serra do Açor mountain range and offers stunning natural surroundings. Visitors can take in breathtaking views of the mountains, valleys, and forests that envelop the village. The area is ideal for hiking, nature walks, and enjoying the tranquility of the countryside.

While Piodão Village doesn't have specific opening and closing times, it is important to note that certain businesses and attractions may have their own operating hours. Restaurants, cafes, and shops within the village typically operate during the day, but their specific hours can vary. It is advisable to check in advance or upon arrival for any specific schedules or to inquire at the local tourism office for up-to-date information.

Piodão Village offers a peaceful and idyllic retreat, allowing visitors to step back in time and immerse themselves in Portugal's traditional rural culture. Its unique architecture, natural beauty, and tranquil atmosphere make it a beloved destination for those seeking an authentic and picturesque experience.

Marvao Village:

A fortified village located in the Alentejo region, known for its impressive castle and walls, as well as stunning views over the surrounding landscape.

Marvão Village, also known as Marvão Castle, is a stunning medieval village located in the Alentejo region of Portugal. Situated on a hilltop in the Serra de São Mamede Natural Park, Marvão is known for its well-preserved fortified walls, panoramic views, and rich historical heritage. While the village itself does not have strict opening and closing times, certain attractions within Marvão have their own operating hours. Here's an overview of Marvão Village:

- Historical Significance: Marvão has a long history dating back to pre-Roman times. The village's strategic location made it an important stronghold for various civilizations, including the Romans, Visigoths, and Moors.

The medieval castle and fortified walls were constructed during the 13th century.

- Castle and Walls: The highlight of Marvão Village is its castle and fortified walls. The castle stands atop the hill, offering panoramic views of the surrounding countryside. Visitors can explore the castle grounds, walk along the fortified walls, and admire the picturesque vistas of the Alentejo region.
- Historic Center: Marvão's historic center is a maze of narrow cobblestone streets, traditional whitewashed houses, and charming squares. Exploring the village on foot allows visitors to soak in the medieval ambiance and discover hidden corners at their own pace.
- Nossa Senhora da Estrela Church: Located within the castle walls, the Nossa Senhora da Estrela Church is a small yet beautiful Romanesque church. It houses valuable religious art and offers a serene space for contemplation.
- Museums and Interpretation Center: Marvão features several small museums and an Interpretation Center that provide insights into the village's history, culture, and natural surroundings. The museums showcase artifacts, traditional crafts, and exhibitions related to the region's heritage.
- Natural Beauty: Marvão is surrounded by stunning natural landscapes. The Serra de São Mamede Natural Park offers opportunities for hiking, birdwatching, and exploring the diverse flora and fauna of the region. Visitors can enjoy scenic walks or venture into the

countryside to appreciate the pristine beauty of the area.

While the village itself doesn't have specific opening and closing times, it is important to note that certain attractions within Marvão, such as museums and churches, may have their own operating hours. Additionally, restaurants, cafes, and shops within the village typically operate during the day. It is advisable to check in advance or upon arrival for any specific schedules or to inquire at the local tourism office for up-to-date information.

Marvão Village's historical charm, breathtaking views, and natural surroundings make it a must-visit destination for travelers seeking a unique and picturesque experience in Portugal.

Castelo Rodrigo Village:

A medieval village located in the Beira region, known for its castle ruins, narrow streets, and well-preserved architecture.

Castelo Rodrigo Village, also known as Castelo Rodrigo, is a historic village located in the north-eastern part of Portugal, near the border with Portugal. Perched on a hilltop, Castelo Rodrigo offers panoramic views of the surrounding countryside and is renowned for its medieval charm, well-preserved architecture, and rich cultural heritage. Here's an overview of Castelo Rodrigo Village:

Historical Significance: Castelo Rodrigo has a long and storied history, with evidence of human settlement dating back to prehistoric times. The village played a significant role in the defense of the Portuguese border during the Middle Ages and was an important frontier fortress against the Spanish kingdom of Castile.

Castle Ruins: The village is crowned by the ruins of a medieval castle, which served as a strategic stronghold. Although much of the castle has been lost to time, visitors can still explore the remains and enjoy breathtaking views from its elevated position.

- Historic Architecture: Castelo Rodrigo's narrow streets are lined with well-preserved medieval houses, displaying traditional architectural features such as stone walls, wooden balconies, and tiled roofs. The village's historical charm extends to its main square, Largo do Pelourinho, where a pillory (pelourinho) stands as a symbol of medieval justice.
- Church of Santiago: The Church of Santiago is a notable religious site in Castelo Rodrigo. This Romanesque church dates back to the 12th century and features a beautiful portal and a unique blend of architectural styles.

- Jewish Quarter: Castelo Rodrigo has a significant Jewish heritage, and the village is home to a well-preserved Jewish quarter. Visitors can explore the narrow streets and discover the remnants of the Jewish community, including a synagogue and Jewish cemetery.
- Natural Surroundings: Castelo Rodrigo is set amidst picturesque natural landscapes, with rolling hills, vineyards, and olive groves surrounding the village. The countryside offers opportunities for hiking, birdwatching, and enjoying the tranquility of rural Portugal.

Visiting Castelo Rodrigo allows travelers to step back in time and experience the historical and cultural richness of the region. The village's medieval architecture, castle ruins, and stunning views make it a captivating destination for those interested in history, architecture, and natural beauty. Whether wandering through its narrow streets, exploring the castle ruins, or simply taking in the panoramic vistas, Castelo Rodrigo Village offers a memorable and authentic experience in Portugal.

Almourol Castle:

A medieval castle located on a small island in the middle of the Tagus River, near the city of Tomar. The castle is accessible by boat and offers stunning views of the surrounding landscape.

Almourol Castle, also known as Castelo de Almourol, is a medieval castle located on a small island in the middle of the Tagus River in Portugal. It is one of the most emblematic and picturesque castles in the country, known for its strategic location, architectural beauty, and rich history. Here's an overview of Almourol Castle:

- Historical Significance: Almourol Castle dates back to the 12th century when it was built by the Knights Templar as a defensive fortress during the Reconquista, the period when Christians reconquered the Iberian Peninsula from the Moors. The castle played a crucial role in the defense of the region and the control of the Tagus River.

- Island Location: Almourol Castle is situated on a small rocky island in the middle of the Tagus River near the town of Vila Nova da Barquinha. The castle's location on an isolated island adds to its charm and makes it a unique and memorable sight.

- Architecture and Features: The castle is a fine example of medieval military architecture. It features sturdy stone walls, battlements, and a keep. The entrance is accessed via a stone bridge that connects the island to the riverbank. Inside the castle, visitors can explore the various levels, climb the towers, and admire the panoramic views of the surrounding landscape.

- Legends and Folklore: Almourol Castle is steeped in legends and folklore. One popular tale tells of a beautiful Moorish princess who lived in the castle and was deeply in love with a Christian knight. The story adds to the castle's romantic allure and captures the imagination of visitors.

- Scenic Surroundings: The castle is set in a picturesque landscape, surrounded by the peaceful waters of the Tagus River and lush greenery. The natural beauty of the area makes it a popular spot for boat trips, where visitors can enjoy scenic views of the castle from the river.

- Visiting Almourol Castle: To reach the castle, visitors can take a short boat ride from the nearby village of Vila Nova da Barquinha. Once on the island, they can explore the castle independently or join guided tours. The castle is open to the public, allowing visitors to immerse themselves in its history and enjoy the panoramic views.

Almourol Castle offers a captivating glimpse into Portugal's medieval past. Its idyllic island location, architectural splendor, and historical significance make it a must-visit destination for history enthusiasts, architecture lovers, and those seeking a unique and picturesque experience in Portugal.

Alcobaca Monastery:

A UNESCO World Heritage Site, this medieval monastery in the Leiria region is famous for its stunning Gothic architecture, including the impressive cloisters and the tombs of King Pedro I and Inês de Castro.

Alcobaça Monastery, also known as Mosteiro de Alcobaça in Portuguese, is a magnificent medieval monastery located in the town of Alcobaça, in central

Portugal. It is one of the most important and impressive examples of Cistercian architecture in the country and holds significant historical and cultural value. Here's an overview of Alcobaça Monastery:

- Historical Significance: Alcobaça Monastery was founded in 1153 by the first Portuguese king, Afonso Henriques, as a gesture of gratitude for the assistance provided by the Cistercian Order during the Reconquista, the Christian reconquest of the Iberian Peninsula. It became the first Cistercian foundation in Portugal and was an important religious, cultural, and political center.
- Architecture: The monastery showcases a stunning blend of Romanesque and Gothic architectural styles. It boasts an impressive façade, intricate rose windows, elegant arches, and a grandiose central nave. The clean lines and simple yet elegant design are characteristic of Cistercian architecture.
- Tombs of Pedro and Inês: Alcobaça Monastery is famous for housing the tombs of Pedro I of Portugal and Inês de Castro, whose tragic love story has become legendary in Portuguese history. The tombs are exquisitely sculpted and intricately detailed, capturing the eternal love between the two.
- Church: The monastery's church, the Church of Santa Maria, is the largest Gothic church in Portugal. Its interior features impressive vaulted ceilings, beautiful stained glass windows, and ornate altarpieces. The church's acoustics are renowned, and it is often used as a venue for concerts and choral performances.

- Cloisters: Alcobaça Monastery boasts two beautiful cloisters, the Gothic Cloister and the Manueline Cloister. The Gothic Cloister is known for its elegant arches and tranquil atmosphere, while the Manueline Cloister showcases intricate stone carvings depicting scenes from everyday life, mythology, and the Age of Discovery.
- Library: The monastery's library contains a valuable collection of ancient manuscripts and illuminated books. Although not accessible to the public, its historical significance contributes to the overall cultural wealth of the monastery.

Visiting Alcobaça Monastery allows travelers to immerse themselves in the rich history and architectural splendor of Portugal. The monastery's grandeur, its connection to the country's early kings, and the renowned love story of Pedro and Inês make it a captivating destination for those interested in Portuguese culture, history, and art.

Peneda-Geres National Park:

The only national park in Portugal, located in the Minho region, offering stunning natural beauty, including mountains, forests, rivers, and wildlife.

Peneda-Gerês National Park, also known as Parque Nacional da Peneda-Gerês in Portuguese, is a vast protected area located in the northern part of Portugal. It is the only national park in the country and covers an area of approximately 700 square kilometers (270 square miles). Peneda-Gerês National Park is known for its stunning natural landscapes, diverse ecosystems, cultural heritage, and outdoor recreational opportunities. Here's an overview of the park:

- Natural Beauty: Peneda-Gerês National Park is characterized by its breathtaking natural beauty. It encompasses rugged mountains, deep valleys, crystal-clear lakes, cascading waterfalls, and dense forests. The park's landscapes are a result of the region's geological history, shaped by glacial activity and erosion over thousands of years.
- Flora and Fauna: The park is home to a wide variety of plant and animal species. Its diverse ecosystems support a rich array of flora, including oak, chestnut, and birch forests, as well as numerous wildflowers and orchids. Wildlife in the park includes the Iberian wolf, roe deer, wild boar, otters, and various bird species, making it an excellent destination for nature lovers and wildlife enthusiasts.
- Cultural Heritage: Peneda-Gerês National Park is not only a natural wonder but also encompasses cultural heritage sites. The park is dotted with traditional villages where locals maintain their traditional way of life, and

visitors can experience the local culture and customs. The park also features ancient Roman roads, prehistoric rock carvings, and historic landmarks such as the medieval Castle of Lindoso.

- Outdoor Activities: The park offers a wide range of outdoor activities for visitors to enjoy. Hiking is particularly popular, with a network of well-marked trails that allow exploration of the park's diverse landscapes. Other activities include mountain biking, horseback riding, birdwatching, and fishing. The park also has designated areas for camping and picnicking.
- Thermal Springs and Waterfalls: Peneda-Gerês National Park is home to several thermal springs and natural waterfalls. The thermal springs, such as the Caldas do Gerês, offer relaxation and therapeutic benefits. Cascata do Arado and Cascata do Tahiti are two of the park's stunning waterfalls that are worth visiting.
- Visitor Centers and Interpretive Exhibitions: The park has visitor centers and interpretive exhibitions that provide information about its natural and cultural heritage. These centers offer educational programs, guided tours, and interactive exhibits to enhance visitors' understanding and appreciation of the park.

Peneda-Gerês National Park offers a unique blend of natural beauty, biodiversity, cultural heritage, and outdoor adventure. Whether you're seeking tranquility amidst pristine nature or engaging in thrilling activities, the park provides a remarkable experience for nature enthusiasts, hikers, and anyone looking to immerse themselves in Portugal's natural wonders.

Evora City:

Évora is a historic city located in the Alentejo region of Portugal. It is known for its rich history, well-preserved architecture, and status as a UNESCO World Heritage site. Évora offers visitors a glimpse into Portugal's past with its ancient Roman ruins, medieval streets, and impressive landmarks. Here's an overview of Évora:

- Historic Center: The heart of Évora is its well-preserved historic center, which has been inhabited for over 2,000 years. The narrow cobbled streets, whitewashed houses, and ancient walls create a charming and timeless ambiance. The historic center is a UNESCO World Heritage site, recognized for its architectural and cultural significance.

- Roman Temple of Évora: One of Évora's most iconic landmarks is the Roman Temple, also known as the Temple of Diana. This well-preserved Roman temple dates back to the 1st century and is an impressive example of ancient Roman architecture in Portugal.
- Cathedral of Évora: The Sé Cathedral is a grand medieval cathedral that dominates the city's skyline. Built between the 13th and 14th centuries, the cathedral showcases a mix of Romanesque and Gothic styles. Inside, visitors can explore the impressive nave, chapels, and the rooftop terrace offering panoramic views of the city.
- Chapel of Bones: The Capela dos Ossos (Chapel of Bones) is a unique attraction in Évora. Located within the Church of São Francisco, the chapel's interior is lined with human bones and skulls, creating a macabre yet intriguing sight. It serves as a reminder of the transitory nature of human existence.
- University of Évora: The University of Évora is one of the oldest universities in Portugal, founded in 1559. It is housed in a magnificent building with beautiful courtyards and gardens. The university has played a significant role in Évora's cultural and intellectual heritage.
- Giraldo Square: Praça do Giraldo is the main square in Évora and a vibrant hub of activity. It is surrounded by historic buildings, shops, cafes, and restaurants. The square is named after Geraldo Geraldes, a Portuguese hero who played a key role in the reconquest of Évora from the Moors.

- Cuisine and Wine: Évora is known for its delicious traditional cuisine and local wines. Visitors can indulge in regional dishes such as açorda (bread soup), migas (fried breadcrumbs with various ingredients), and traditional Alentejo wines.

Évora offers a captivating blend of history, culture, and gastronomy. Its well-preserved architectural heritage, ancient ruins, and vibrant atmosphere make it a popular destination for tourists seeking an authentic Portuguese experience. Whether wandering through the narrow streets, visiting historic landmarks, or savoring the local cuisine, Évora provides a delightful journey into Portugal's past.

Belmonte Village:

A charming village located in the Serra da Estrela mountain range, known for its well-preserved Jewish quarter, the beautiful castle, and the museum dedicated to the Jewish heritage.

Belmonte is a charming village located in the Castelo Branco District of Portugal. Nestled in the foothills of the Serra da Estrela mountain range, Belmonte is known for its rich Jewish heritage, historical significance, and beautiful natural surroundings. Here's an overview of Belmonte Village:

- Jewish Heritage: Belmonte is particularly renowned for its Jewish heritage. It is home to one of the oldest Jewish communities in Portugal, which has maintained its traditions and customs throughout the centuries. Visitors can explore the Jewish Museum of Belmonte, which provides insights into the history, culture, and traditions of the Sephardic Jews.

- Belmonte Castle: The village is dominated by Belmonte Castle, a medieval fortress perched on a hilltop. The castle dates back to the 13th century and offers panoramic views of the surrounding landscape. Inside, visitors can discover the castle's history through exhibitions and explore the tower, walls, and battlements.

- Church of Santiago: The Church of Santiago is a significant religious site in Belmonte. It dates back to the 13th century and features a mix of architectural styles, including Romanesque and Gothic. The church houses beautiful altarpieces and religious artifacts.

- Historical Center: Belmonte's historic center is a delightful place to wander. The narrow, winding streets are lined with traditional houses adorned with wrought-iron balconies and colorful window frames. The atmosphere is tranquil and invites exploration.

- Natural Beauty: Belmonte is surrounded by beautiful natural landscapes. The village is located near the Serra da Estrela Natural Park, offering opportunities for hiking, nature walks, and outdoor activities. The park features picturesque mountains, valleys, and rivers, making it a paradise for nature lovers.

- Olive Oil Production: Belmonte is known for its olive oil production. Visitors can learn about the traditional methods of olive oil extraction and even participate in tastings and tours of local olive oil mills.
- Cultural Events: Belmonte hosts various cultural events throughout the year, celebrating the village's heritage and traditions. These events include festivals, exhibitions, and performances that showcase the local culture, music, and crafts.

Belmonte Village offers a unique blend of history, cultural heritage, and natural beauty. Its Jewish heritage, medieval castle, and scenic surroundings make it a captivating destination for history enthusiasts, nature lovers, and those seeking an authentic Portuguese experience. Whether exploring the village's historical sites, immersing oneself in the local traditions, or enjoying the natural landscapes, Belmonte provides a memorable journey into the heart of Portugal.

Montesinho Natural Park:

A beautiful natural park located in the Tras-os-Montes region, known for its stunning mountains, rivers, and wildlife, as well as the traditional rural lifestyle of the local communities.

Montesinho Natural Park, or Parque Natural de Montesinho in Portuguese, is a protected area located in the northeastern part of Portugal, near the border with Portugal. Covering an area of approximately 75,000 hectares, Montesinho Natural Park is known for its pristine landscapes, diverse flora and fauna, traditional rural communities, and outdoor recreational opportunities. Here's an overview of Montesinho Natural Park:

- Natural Beauty: Montesinho Natural Park is characterized by its rugged mountains, deep valleys, dense forests, and meandering rivers. The park showcases a diverse range of landscapes, including granite peaks, rolling hills, and picturesque streams. Its natural beauty provides a haven for outdoor enthusiasts and nature lovers.
- Biodiversity: The park is home to a rich variety of plant and animal species. Its forests consist of oak, chestnut, and pine trees, providing habitat for several species of birds, mammals, reptiles, and amphibians. Rare and endangered species, such as the Iberian wolf and the golden eagle, can also be found in the park.
- Hiking and Outdoor Activities: Montesinho Natural Park offers numerous hiking trails that allow visitors to explore its diverse landscapes. The trails range from easy walks to more challenging hikes, offering breathtaking views and opportunities to observe wildlife. The park is also suitable for other outdoor activities such as birdwatching, mountain biking, and nature photography.
- Traditional Rural Communities: The park is home to several traditional rural communities where traditional ways of life and cultural

practices are preserved. The villages within the park, such as Montesinho and Rio de Onor, provide an opportunity to experience the local culture, traditional architecture, and authentic cuisine.

- Cultural Heritage: Montesinho Natural Park is not only a haven for nature but also showcases the region's cultural heritage. Visitors can explore ancient stone ruins, traditional watermills, and shepherds' huts that reflect the historical and cultural significance of the area.

- Local Gastronomy: The park is known for its delicious traditional cuisine, which often features local products and specialties. Visitors can indulge in regional dishes such as hearty stews, sausages, smoked meats, and local cheeses. The local gastronomy provides a true taste of the region's culinary heritage.

Montesinho Natural Park offers a peaceful and immersive experience in the heart of nature. Its stunning landscapes, biodiversity, traditional rural communities, and cultural heritage make it an ideal destination for those seeking tranquility, outdoor adventures, and an authentic Portuguese experience.

Sortelha Village:

A medieval village located in the Beira region, known for its well-preserved castle, walls, and houses built with local granite stones.

Sortelha is a picturesque medieval village located in the Guarda District of Portugal. It is renowned for its well-preserved medieval architecture, ancient walls, and panoramic views of the surrounding countryside. Sortelha is often referred to as a living museum, as it offers visitors a glimpse into the past with its historic charm and well-maintained buildings. Here's an overview of Sortelha Village:

- Historical Significance: Sortelha has a history that dates back to Roman times, and its medieval origins are still evident in its architecture and layout. The village played a strategic role in the region's defense, with its fortified walls and hilltop location providing a vantage point against potential invaders.

- Medieval Walls and Castle: The village is encircled by medieval walls, which are remarkably intact. Walking along the walls offers panoramic views of the surrounding countryside, including the Côa Valley and the Serra da Estrela mountain range. The village's medieval castle, located at the highest point, adds to the historic ambiance.

- Traditional Houses: Sortelha is characterized by its traditional granite houses with their stone facades, wooden balconies, and slate roofs. These well-preserved houses create a charming atmosphere and provide a sense of stepping back in time.

- Historic Landmarks: Within the village, visitors can explore the Church of Santa Maria, a small but beautiful Romanesque church with unique architectural details. There is also a pillory, a symbol of municipal power and justice in medieval times, and a charming central square with a fountain.

- Rural Surroundings: Sortelha is surrounded by a rural landscape of rolling hills, olive groves, and vineyards. The countryside offers opportunities for outdoor activities such as hiking, biking, and exploring the region's natural beauty.

- Local Culture and Traditions: Sortelha celebrates its cultural heritage through various events and festivals, which provide insights into local traditions, crafts, and gastronomy. These events often showcase traditional music, dance, and culinary specialties.

Visiting Sortelha Village allows travelers to immerse themselves in the medieval atmosphere and architectural beauty of the region. The well-preserved walls, castle, and traditional houses, combined with the stunning natural surroundings, make Sortelha a captivating destination for history enthusiasts, architecture lovers, and those seeking a unique and tranquil experience in Portugal.

Chapter 4.
Itineraries

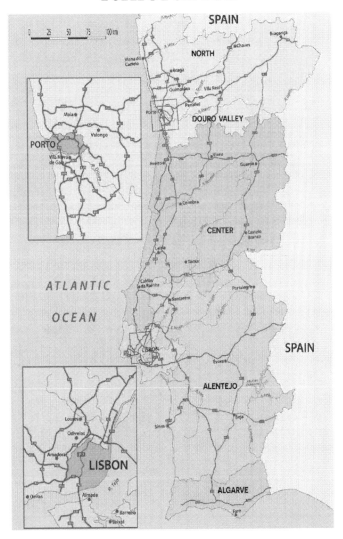

ALENTEJO

82

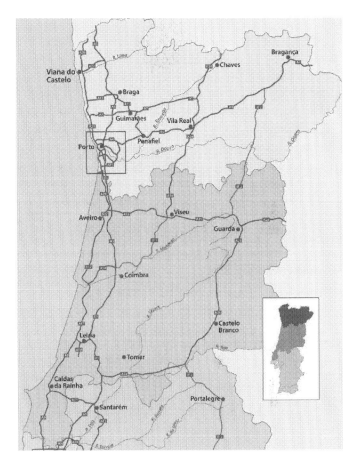

Whether you have just a weekend or several weeks to explore Portugal, there are many different itineraries that you can choose from. Some popular options include:

- Lisbon and Porto: These two cities are the largest in Portugal and offer a great introduction to the country's history, culture, and cuisine. Spend a few days in each city,

83

exploring the historic neighborhoods, museums, and restaurants.

- Algarve Beaches: If you're looking for sun, sand, and relaxation, the Algarve region in the south of Portugal is the perfect destination. Spend a week exploring the region's beautiful beaches, picturesque towns, and delicious seafood.
- Douro Valley: The Douro Valley is one of the most scenic regions in Portugal, with terraced vineyards, historic wine estates, and charming villages. Spend a few days exploring the valley before heading to Porto to sample the city's famous port wine.

Therefore, you may want to tailor this itinerary to your specific interests and travel schedule.

7 day Itinerary

Day 1: Lisbon

Explore the historic Alfama neighborhood and visit the Lisbon Cathedral

Take a tram ride through the city

Visit the iconic Belem Tower and Jeronimos Monastery

Watch the sunset from the Miradouro da Senhora do Monte viewpoint

Day 2: Sintra and Cascais

Take a day trip to Sintra, a picturesque town known for its fairy tale castles and palaces

Visit the famous Pena Palace and the Moorish Castle

Head to the coastal town of Cascais for some beach time and seafood dinner

Day 3: Coimbra

Head north to Coimbra, a charming university city with a rich history

Visit the stunning Coimbra University and the Biblioteca Joanina library

Explore the narrow streets and alleys of the old town

Day 4: Porto

Head to Porto, the second largest city in Portugal

Take a stroll along the Ribeira, the historic riverfront district

Visit the iconic Dom Luis I Bridge and the Porto Cathedral

Sample some of the famous port wine at one of the many cellars in Vila Nova de Gaia

Day 5: Douro Valley

Take a day trip to the Douro Valley, a UNESCO World Heritage site known for its vineyards and stunning scenery

Take a boat ride along the Douro River and visit some of the local wineries for wine tastings

Enjoy a traditional Portuguese lunch in one of the small towns along the way

Day 6: Algarve

Head south to the Algarve region, known for its stunning beaches and coastline

Visit the famous Ponta da Piedade cliffs and caves near Lagos

Relax on the beautiful beaches of Albufeira or Faro

Day 7: Lisbon

Return to Lisbon for your final day in Portugal

Take a day trip to the nearby town of Sintra or the fishing village of Cascais

Explore the trendy neighborhoods of Bairro Alto and Chiado

Enjoy a traditional Portuguese dinner with fado music to end your trip on a high note.

3 day itinerary in Portugal

Day 1: Lisbon

Explore the historic Alfama neighborhood and visit the Lisbon Cathedral

Take a tram ride through the city

Visit the iconic Belem Tower and Jeronimos Monastery

Watch the sunset from the Miradouro da Senhora do Monte viewpoint

Day 2: Sintra and Cascais

Take a day trip to Sintra, a picturesque town known for its fairy tale castles and palaces

Visit the famous Pena Palace and the Moorish Castle

Head to the coastal town of Cascais for some beach time and seafood dinner

Day 3: Porto

Head to Porto, the second largest city in Portugal

Take a stroll along the Ribeira, the historic riverfront district

Visit the iconic Dom Luis I Bridge and the Porto Cathedral

Sample some of the famous port wine at one of the many cellars in Vila Nova de Gaia

Alternatively, if you want to focus on a specific region, you could do:

Day 1: Lisbon

Explore the historic Alfama neighborhood and visit the Lisbon Cathedral

Take a tram ride through the city

Visit the iconic Belem Tower and Jeronimos Monastery

Watch the sunset from the Miradouro da Senhora do Monte viewpoint

Day 2: Sintra and Cascais

Take a day trip to Sintra, a picturesque town known for its fairy tale castles and palaces

Visit the famous Pena Palace and the Moorish Castle

Head to the coastal town of Cascais for some beach time and seafood dinner

Day 3: Algarve

Head south to the Algarve region, known for its stunning beaches and coastline

Visit the famous Ponta da Piedade cliffs and caves near Lagos

Relax on the beautiful beaches of Albufeira or Faro

Keep in mind that Portugal is a diverse country with many wonderful cities and sights to explore, so this itinerary can be tailored to your specific interests and travel schedule.

7 day itinerary in Portugal

Day 1: Lisbon

Explore the historic Alfama neighborhood and visit the Lisbon Cathedral

Take a tram ride through the city

Visit the iconic Belem Tower and Jeronimos Monastery

Watch the sunset from the Miradouro da Senhora do Monte viewpoint

Day 2: Sintra and Cascais

Take a day trip to Sintra, a picturesque town known for its fairy tale castles and palaces

Visit the famous Pena Palace and the Moorish Castle

Head to the coastal town of Cascais for some beach time and seafood dinner

Day 3: Coimbra

Head north to Coimbra, a charming university city with a rich history

Visit the stunning Coimbra University and the Biblioteca Joanina library

Explore the narrow streets and alleys of the old town

Day 4: Porto

Head to Porto, the second largest city in Portugal

Take a stroll along the Ribeira, the historic riverfront district

Visit the iconic Dom Luis I Bridge and the Porto Cathedral

Sample some of the famous port wine at one of the many cellars in Vila Nova de Gaia

Day 5: Douro Valley

Take a day trip to the Douro Valley, a UNESCO World Heritage site known for its vineyards and stunning scenery

Take a boat ride along the Douro River and visit some of the local wineries for wine tastings

Enjoy a traditional Portuguese lunch in one of the small towns along the way

Day 6: Algarve

Head south to the Algarve region, known for its stunning beaches and coastline

Visit the famous Ponta da Piedade cliffs and caves near Lagos

Relax on the beautiful beaches of Albufeira or Faro

Day 7: Lisbon

Return to Lisbon for your final day in Portugal

Take a day trip to the nearby town of Sintra or the fishing village of Cascais

Explore the trendy neighborhoods of Bairro Alto and Chiado

Enjoy a traditional Portuguese dinner with fado music to end your trip on a high note.

14 day itinerary in Portugal

Day 1: Lisbon

Explore the historic Alfama neighborhood and visit the Lisbon Cathedral

Take a tram ride through the city

Visit the iconic Belem Tower and Jeronimos Monastery

Watch the sunset from the Miradouro da Senhora do Monte viewpoint

Day 2: Sintra and Cascais

Take a day trip to Sintra, a picturesque town known for its fairy tale castles and palaces

Visit the famous Pena Palace and the Moorish Castle

Head to the coastal town of Cascais for some beach time and seafood dinner

Day 3: Coimbra

Head north to Coimbra, a charming university city with a rich history

Visit the stunning Coimbra University and the Biblioteca Joanina library

Explore the narrow streets and alleys of the old town

Day 4-5: Porto

Head to Porto, the second largest city in Portugal

Take a stroll along the Ribeira, the historic riverfront district

Visit the iconic Dom Luis I Bridge and the Porto Cathedral

Sample some of the famous port wine at one of the many cellars in Vila Nova de Gaia

Take a day trip to the Douro Valley, a UNESCO World Heritage site known for its vineyards and stunning scenery

Take a boat ride along the Douro River and visit some of the local wineries for wine tastings

Enjoy a traditional Portuguese lunch in one of the small towns along the way

Day 6-7: Aveiro and Costa Nova

Head to Aveiro, a charming town known as the Venice of Portugal, and take a boat ride along the canals

Visit the colorful striped houses of Costa Nova and enjoy the beach

Sample the traditional sweet egg pastries known as "ovos moles"

Day 8-9: Alentejo Region

Head south to the Alentejo region, known for its stunning countryside and vineyards

Visit the medieval town of Evora and its Roman ruins

Explore the wine estates and sample the local wines

Take a hot air balloon ride for a unique perspective of the region

Day 10-11: Algarve

Head further south to the Algarve region, known for its stunning beaches and coastline

Visit the famous Ponta da Piedade cliffs and caves near Lagos

Relax on the beautiful beaches of Albufeira or Faro

Take a boat tour to see dolphins or explore the Ria Formosa natural park

Day 12-13: Madeira Island

Take a short flight to Madeira Island, known for its natural beauty and mild climate

Explore the capital city of Funchal and its historic center

Take a cable car ride to the village of Monte for stunning views

Visit the botanical gardens and sample the Madeira wine

Day 14: Lisbon

Return to Lisbon for your final day in Portugal

Take a day trip to the nearby town of Sintra or the fishing village of Cascais

Explore the trendy neighborhoods of Bairro Alto and Chiado

Enjoy a traditional Portuguese dinner with fado music to end your trip on a high note.

The best to go sightseeing

Here are some of the best places to go sightseeing in Portugal:

- Lisbon: The capital city of Portugal is a must-visit for any traveler. It's a city filled with historic sites, museums, and galleries. Visit the Belem Tower, the Jeronimos Monastery, and the Castle of Sao Jorge for a glimpse into Portugal's history.
- Porto: Known for its stunning architecture, Port wine, and the Douro River, Porto is a charming city that is worth visiting. Make sure to visit the Ribeira district, the Clérigos Tower, and the Palácio da Bolsa.
- Sintra: A UNESCO World Heritage Site, Sintra is a magical town located just outside Lisbon. It's known for its stunning palaces, including the Palacio da Pena and the Quinta da Regaleira.
- Algarve: Located in the southern region of Portugal, the Algarve is known for its beautiful beaches, golf courses, and coastal towns. Make sure to visit Lagos, Albufeira, and Faro.
- Coimbra: Home to one of the oldest universities in Europe, Coimbra is a charming city with a rich history. Visit the University of Coimbra, the Joanina Library, and the Old Cathedral.
- Évora: Located in the Alentejo region of Portugal, Évora is a well-preserved medieval town. Visit the Temple of Diana, the Sé Cathedral, and the Chapel of Bones.
- Madeira: This island paradise is located off the coast of Portugal and is known for its stunning scenery and mild climate. Visit Funchal, the

capital city, and take a cable car ride to the Monte Palace Tropical Garden.

- Azores: A group of islands located in the middle of the Atlantic Ocean, the Azores are known for their natural beauty and unique culture. Visit the island of Sao Miguel for its stunning crater lakes, hot springs, and traditional villages.

- These are just a few of the many places to go sightseeing in Portugal. With its rich history, stunning landscapes, and vibrant culture, Portugal is a destination that should be on every traveler's list.

- Guimarães: Known as the birthplace of Portugal, Guimarães is a historic city that played a significant role in Portugal's history. Visit the Guimarães Castle, the Palace of the Dukes of Bragança, and the beautiful historic center.

- Tomar: Located in central Portugal, Tomar is a small town with a rich history. Visit the Convent of Christ, a UNESCO World Heritage Site that was once the headquarters of the Knights Templar.

- Obidos: This charming medieval town is located north of Lisbon and is known for its well-preserved castle walls and picturesque streets. Visit the Castle of Obidos, the Church of Santa Maria, and try the famous cherry liqueur, Ginja.

- Aveiro: Known as the "Venice of Portugal," Aveiro is a picturesque town with canals, colorful boats, and beautiful Art Nouveau buildings. Take a boat ride along the canals, visit the Aveiro Museum, and try the local specialty, ovos moles.

- Braga: Known as the "Rome of Portugal," Braga is a historic city with many churches and religious sites. Visit the Braga Cathedral, the Bom Jesus do Monte Sanctuary, and the Santa Barbara Garden.
- Viana do Castelo: This seaside town is located in the north of Portugal and is known for its beautiful beaches, traditional festivals, and historic architecture. Visit the Basilica of Santa Luzia, the Gil Eannes Ship Museum, and the Cabedelo Beach.
- Monsanto: This historic village is located in central Portugal and is known for its unique architecture, as the houses are built around boulders and rocks. Visit the Castle of Monsanto, the Chapel of Saint Anthony, and the Miradouro de Monsanto viewpoint.

Mistakes to avoid to save time and money while traveling in Portugal

To make the most of your trip to Portugal, here are a few tips to keep in mind:

- Purchase tickets in advance for museums and monuments to skip the lines.
- Watch out for pickpockets in crowded tourist areas, especially in Lisbon and Porto.
- Not researching transportation options: Portugal has a good public transportation system, including trains, buses, and metros, which can be a cost-effective way to get around. However, it's important to research the different options, routes, and schedules to avoid wasting time and money.
- Overpacking: It can be tempting to bring everything you might need on your trip, but

overpacking can lead to additional baggage fees, difficulty in moving around, and the hassle of carrying heavy luggage. Pack light and prioritize essential items.

- Not using local currency: While many places in Portugal accept credit cards, it's a good idea to have some local currency on hand for smaller purchases, public transportation, and tipping.

- Eating in touristy areas: Eating in popular tourist areas can be significantly more expensive than eating at local restaurants. Look for authentic Portuguese restaurants, cafes, and markets to get a taste of the local cuisine at a more reasonable price.

- Not planning ahead: Portugal is a popular destination, especially during peak tourist seasons. Make sure to book accommodations, tours, and activities ahead of time to avoid higher prices and availability issues.

- Overlooking free activities: Portugal has many free and low-cost activities, including museums, parks, and festivals. Do some research to find these hidden gems and save money while enjoying your trip.

- Not taking advantage of discounts: If you're a student, senior citizen, or have a disability, you may be eligible for discounts on transportation, attractions, and accommodations. Always ask if there are any available discounts, as it can save you a lot of money in the long run.

- Not being mindful of pickpockets: Like many popular tourist destinations, pickpocketing can be a problem in Portugal. Make sure to keep an eye on your belongings and avoid carrying valuables in easily accessible pockets or bags.

- Only visiting popular destinations: While Lisbon and Porto are must-see destinations, there are many other hidden gems in Portugal that are worth exploring. Consider visiting smaller towns and villages to get a taste of traditional Portuguese culture and avoid the crowds.
- Not trying local wines: Portugal is known for its wine, and many local varieties can be found at affordable prices. Don't be afraid to ask for recommendations or try something new.

Chapter 5.
The local culture

Connecting with the local culture of Portugal is an excellent way to immerse yourself in the country's rich heritage and vibrant atmosphere. Here are some suggestions on how to engage with the local culture in Portugal:

- Explore Local Markets: Visiting local markets is a fantastic way to experience the authentic flavors, sights, and sounds of Portugal. Whether it's the Mercado da Ribeira in Lisbon or Mercado do Bolhão in Porto, you can discover fresh produce, traditional handicrafts, and delicious local specialties. Engage with the vendors, try regional products, and soak up the bustling atmosphere.
- Attend Local Events: Portugal hosts a myriad of cultural events throughout the year, offering an opportunity to connect with the

local community. Look out for festivals, fairs, and religious celebrations like the Festas de Lisboa in June or the Festa de São João in Porto. These events showcase traditional music, dance, costumes, and local customs, allowing you to experience the authentic spirit of Portugal.

- Visit Museums and Historical Sites: Portugal boasts a wealth of museums and historical sites that offer insights into the country's fascinating past. Explore iconic landmarks such as the Tower of Belém in Lisbon, the Jerónimos Monastery, or the Castle of São Jorge. Additionally, museums like the National Museum of Ancient Art or the Museu Nacional do Azulejo provide a deeper understanding of Portuguese art, history, and culture.

- Discover Portuguese Music and Dance: Fado, Portugal's traditional music genre, is deeply ingrained in the country's culture. Attend a live Fado performance in Lisbon's Alfama neighborhood or Coimbra to experience the melancholic melodies and heartfelt lyrics. You can also explore other musical styles like traditional folk music or modern genres such as Portuguese hip-hop. Dance forms like the Vira or the Corridinho offer a glimpse into regional dances.

- Taste Local Cuisine: Portuguese cuisine is diverse, flavorful, and a true reflection of the country's cultural identity. Indulge in iconic dishes such as bacalhau (salted codfish), pastéis de nata (custard tarts), and francesinha (a hearty sandwich). Seek out traditional taverns, known as tasquinhas, to savor regional specialties and engage in conversations with locals. Join a food tour or cooking class to deepen your culinary experience and learn about the local ingredients and cooking techniques.

- Engage with the Local Community: One of the best ways to connect with the local culture is to engage with the Portuguese people themselves. Strike up conversations, learn a few basic Portuguese phrases, and show interest in their traditions and customs. Participate in local workshops or cultural activities organized by community centers or tourist offices to get involved and interact with locals.

Remember to be respectful of local customs, traditions, and etiquette while engaging with the local culture. Embrace the opportunity to learn, appreciate, and celebrate the unique heritage of Portugal.

Best tips for avoiding crowds in Portugal

If you prefer to explore Portugal without large crowds, here are some tips to help you avoid the busiest tourist areas and enjoy a more peaceful experience:

- Visit Off-Season: Consider traveling to Portugal during the shoulder seasons (spring and fall) when the weather is still pleasant, but the number of tourists is generally lower. This way, you can enjoy popular attractions without the overwhelming crowds. Additionally, weekdays tend to be less busy than weekends.
- Explore Lesser-Known Destinations: Portugal is filled with charming towns and villages that are often overlooked by mass tourism. Instead of focusing solely on popular cities like Lisbon

and Porto, venture off the beaten path and visit places such as Évora, Braga, Guimarães, or Aveiro. These destinations offer authentic experiences and are often less crowded.

- Plan Your Sightseeing: Research the popular attractions and plan your visits strategically. Arriving early in the morning or late in the afternoon can help you avoid the peak hours when crowds tend to be at their highest. Some attractions also have extended hours on certain days, providing an opportunity to explore when there are fewer visitors.

- Explore Nature and Rural Areas: Portugal is blessed with breathtaking natural landscapes and countryside. Consider exploring national parks, coastal areas, and rural regions where you can enjoy tranquility and escape the crowds. Places like Peneda-Gerês National Park, the Alentejo region, or the Douro Valley offer beautiful scenery and a quieter atmosphere.

- Opt for Smaller Accommodations: Instead of staying in large hotels or resorts, consider boutique hotels, guesthouses, or bed and breakfasts. These smaller accommodations are often located in quieter neighborhoods or more secluded areas, providing a peaceful retreat after a day of exploring.

- Use Alternative Transportation: Public transportation can get crowded during peak hours, especially in major cities. To avoid the rush, consider exploring on foot, renting a bike, or using alternative modes of transportation like tuk-tuks or electric scooters. These options allow you to navigate through the streets at your own pace and explore lesser-known areas.

- Seek Local Recommendations: Interacting with locals can provide valuable insights into lesser-known places and hidden gems that are off the tourist radar. Strike up conversations with locals, ask for recommendations, and explore their favorite local spots. They can point you towards authentic experiences that are less crowded.
- Try local cuisine: Avoid tourist traps by trying local cuisine at local restaurants instead of eating at touristy places. Ask locals for recommendations on the best places to eat.
- Learn some basic Portuguese: While many Portuguese people speak English, learning some basic Portuguese phrases can be helpful when communicating with locals. It can also show that you have made an effort to immerse yourself in the local culture.
- Take advantage of free walking tours: Many cities in Portugal offer free walking tours that are led by knowledgeable local guides. These tours are a great way to learn about the history and culture of a city and can often take you to off-the-beaten-path locations.
- Visit museums on free admission days: Many museums in Portugal offer free admission on certain days of the week or month. Research these days in advance and plan your museum visits accordingly to save money and avoid crowds.
- Avoid touristy souvenir shops: Instead of buying souvenirs at touristy souvenir shops, try shopping at local markets or artisanal shops for unique and authentic souvenirs.

Remember to check the opening hours and availability of attractions or activities in advance, as some may have limited access or require pre-booking. By planning ahead, exploring lesser-known areas, and embracing a more relaxed pace of travel, you can enjoy Portugal while avoiding the crowds and savoring a more intimate experience.

The best restaurants, clubs and nightlife in Portugal

Portugal offers a vibrant and diverse culinary and nightlife scene. Here are some popular restaurants, clubs, and nightlife destinations worth exploring in the country:

Restaurants:

Belcanto (Lisbon): A Michelin-starred restaurant led by renowned chef José Avillez, offering a sophisticated and innovative Portuguese dining experience.

O Paparico (Porto): Known for its traditional Portuguese cuisine with a modern twist, using high-quality ingredients and offering a warm and welcoming atmosphere.

Cervejaria Ramiro (Lisbon): A legendary seafood restaurant serving the freshest seafood and shellfish in a lively and bustling environment.

Taberna do Mercado (Lisbon): Chef Nuno Mendes combines Portuguese flavors with a contemporary twist, offering a casual and relaxed dining experience.

A Cozinha da Maria (Porto): A small, family-run restaurant serving delicious home-style Portuguese dishes with a focus on local ingredients.

Here are some low-cost restaurants in popular cities across Portugal:

Low budget

Lisbon:

A Baiuca: This small tasca in the Alfama district serves traditional Portuguese dishes at affordable prices, with live Fado music in the evenings.

Cervejaria Ramiro: Known for its seafood, this popular spot offers reasonably priced dishes like shrimp, crab, and clams.

O Prego da Peixaria: Famous for its prego (steak sandwich), this casual eatery serves delicious sandwiches at budget-friendly prices.

Porto:

Conga: Located near the Bolhão Market, Conga is renowned for its bifanas (pork sandwiches) and francesinhas (a hearty sandwich with layers of meat, cheese, and sauce).

Gazela: This unassuming restaurant in the city center is known for its francesinhas, as well as other affordable Portuguese classics.

Casa Guedes: Famous for its slow-roasted pork sandwiches, Casa Guedes is a local favorite offering excellent value for money.

Faro:

Adega Nova: Located in the historic center, this restaurant serves traditional Algarve cuisine at reasonable prices, including fresh seafood and cataplana (a regional seafood stew).

Restaurante Zé Maria: A family-owned eatery known for its generous portions and affordable prices, offering a variety of Portuguese dishes.

Coimbra:

A Cozinha da Maria: This cozy restaurant near the university serves homemade-style Portuguese dishes, including daily specials at affordable prices.

O Pátio: A popular local spot that offers a buffet-style lunch with a variety of dishes, including vegetarian options, at budget-friendly rates.

Albufeira:

O Manel dos Frangos: Specializing in grilled chicken, this restaurant offers delicious and affordable meals, along with sides like fries and salad.

A Ruina: Located in the Old Town, A Ruina serves traditional Portuguese cuisine with a focus on fresh fish and seafood at reasonable prices.

These are just a few examples, but you'll find many more low-cost restaurants in each city. Exploring the local neighborhoods and seeking recommendations from locals or online sources will help you discover hidden gems that suit your budget while providing an authentic dining experience.

High-cost restaurants in popular cities across Portugal:

Lisbon:

Belcanto: A Michelin two-star restaurant helmed by chef José Avillez, offering an innovative and sophisticated dining experience with a focus on Portuguese cuisine.

Eleven: Located on top of Edward VII Park, Eleven is a Michelin-starred restaurant known for its panoramic views of the city and contemporary Portuguese cuisine.

Porto:

The Yeatman: A luxurious hotel with a Michelin-starred restaurant overlooking the Douro River, offering an exquisite dining experience featuring traditional Portuguese flavors.

Pedro Lemos: A Michelin-starred restaurant in Foz do Douro, known for its creative and refined dishes using local ingredients.

Faro:

Vila Joya: Situated in a luxury boutique hotel in Albufeira, Vila Joya is a two-Michelin-starred restaurant with a focus on modern European cuisine prepared with local ingredients.

Coimbra:

Arcadas da Capela: Located in the luxurious Hotel Quinta das Lágrimas, this Michelin-starred restaurant combines contemporary cuisine with traditional Portuguese flavors in an elegant setting.

Albufeira:

São Gabriel: A Michelin-starred restaurant in Vale do Lobo, São Gabriel offers an exquisite fine dining experience with a focus on Mediterranean cuisine and seasonal ingredients.

It's important to note that high-cost restaurants offer exceptional culinary experiences but may come with higher price tags. Reservations are often recommended for these establishments, especially during peak tourist seasons. Keep in mind that these recommendations may change over time, so it's best to check for up-to-date information and reviews before making a reservation.

Clubs and Nightlife:

Portugal offers a vibrant nightlife scene with a variety of clubs, pubs, and activities in different cities. Here's a glimpse of the nightlife in some popular cities:

Lisbon:

Bairro Alto: This neighborhood comes alive at night with its narrow streets filled with bars, pubs, and small clubs. It's a popular spot for bar-hopping and enjoying live music.

Lux Fragil: One of Lisbon's most famous nightclubs, located by the Tagus River. It attracts renowned DJs and offers different dance floors and music styles.

Park Bar: Situated on top of a parking garage, this rooftop bar offers stunning views of the city and a relaxed atmosphere.

Porto:

Ribeira District: This area is known for its lively atmosphere, with bars and restaurants lining the streets along the Douro River. It's a great place for drinks, live music, and socializing.

Maus Hábitos: A multi-purpose cultural space that hosts live music, art exhibitions, and DJ sets. It has a rooftop terrace with a bar and offers a unique and alternative nightlife experience.

Gare Club: Located in a renovated train station, Gare Club is a popular venue for electronic music lovers and hosts both local and international DJs.

Faro:

The Strip: Located in the Albufeira district, The Strip is a long street filled with bars, clubs, and restaurants, offering a vibrant nightlife atmosphere.

Club Heaven: A popular nightclub with multiple dance floors and a variety of music genres, including house, R&B, and hip-hop.

NoSoloÁgua Vilamoura: Situated on Vilamoura Beach, this beach club offers a mix of daytime beach activities and nighttime parties with DJs, cocktails, and a lively atmosphere.

Coimbra:

Praça da República: The main square in Coimbra, also known as "República," is lined with bars and nightclubs. It's a popular spot for students and young locals to gather and socialize.

NB Club: Located in the city center, NB Club is a popular nightclub featuring a variety of music genres and hosting themed parties and events.

Each city in Portugal has its own unique nightlife offerings, and it's always a good idea to explore local recommendations and ask for suggestions based on your specific interests. It's worth noting that nightlife options may vary depending on the day of the week and the time of the year, so it's advisable to check for events and opening hours in advance.

More clubs

Lux Frágil (Lisbon): One of the most renowned clubs in Portugal, known for its eclectic music selection and stunning views of the Tagus River.

Pacha Ofir (Ofir): Situated on the northern coast, this club hosts top DJs and offers an unforgettable beachside party experience.

Maus Hábitos (Porto): A cultural and artistic hub with a rooftop bar, gallery, and club, showcasing a mix of music styles and art exhibitions.

NoSoloÁgua (Portimão): A beachfront lounge and club offering a vibrant atmosphere, live music, and DJ performances right by the sea.

Kremlin (Lisbon): A popular LGBT-friendly club with multiple dance floors, featuring a mix of music genres and hosting various themed parties.

Note that the nightlife scene can vary depending on the city and the time of year. It's always a good idea to check for any events or parties happening during your visit to make the most of the nightlife experience in Portugal.

List of typical foods and drinks to try during a trip to Portugal

During your trip to Portugal, make sure to try these typical foods and drinks to experience the rich culinary culture of the country:

Bacalhau à Brás: A traditional Portuguese dish made with salted codfish, eggs, onions, and thin potato fries.

Pastéis de Nata: These creamy custard tarts with a flaky pastry crust are a must-try Portuguese treat. They are often enjoyed with a sprinkle of cinnamon or powdered sugar.

Francesinha: Originating from Porto, this hearty sandwich consists of layers of different meats (such as ham, steak, and sausage) covered in melted cheese and a rich tomato and beer sauce. Caldo Verde: A comforting soup made with kale, potatoes, onions, and slices of chorizo sausage. It is a popular dish, particularly in the colder months.

Piri-Piri Chicken: Grilled or roasted chicken marinated in a spicy piri-piri sauce made from hot chili peppers. It's a flavorful and popular dish in Portugal.

Sardinhas Assadas: Grilled sardines are a Portuguese summertime delicacy, particularly during the popular Santo António and São João festivals. Arroz de Marisco: A flavorful seafood rice dish cooked with a variety of shellfish like shrimp, clams, mussels, and sometimes crab or lobster.

Pastel de Bacalhau: These fried codfish cakes are crispy on the outside and tender on the inside. They make for a delicious appetizer or snack. Vinho Verde: Portugal's famous "green wine" is a light and refreshing white or rosé wine, often slightly sparkling. It pairs well with seafood and warm weather.

Port Wine: A sweet and fortified wine produced in the Douro Valley region. Port wine comes in different styles and can be enjoyed as an aperitif or paired with desserts. Ginjinha: A sour cherry liqueur known as Ginja, typically served in small chocolate cups. It's a popular digestif and a symbol of Lisbon's traditional drinking culture.. Bifanas: Thinly sliced marinated pork loin sandwiches, often enjoyed with mustard or hot sauce. They are a popular street food option in Portugal. These are just a few examples of the delicious and distinctive foods and drinks you can try during your visit to Portugal. Make sure to explore local markets, traditional taverns, and recommended restaurants to savor the authentic flavors of the country.

Chapter 6.
Accommodation

Portugal offers a wide range of accommodations to suit various budgets and preferences. Whether you're looking for affordable options or luxury hotels, here are some recommendations for places to stay during your trip to Portugal:

Lisbon:

Budget: Lisbon offers numerous budget-friendly accommodations, including hostels and guesthouses in areas like Baixa, Alfama, and Bairro Alto. Some popular budget options include Travellers House, Goodmorning Hostel, and Lisbon Chillout Hostel.

Mid-range: For a comfortable stay with additional amenities, consider mid-range hotels such as Hotel Santa Justa, Lisbon Arsenal Suites, or LX Boutique Hotel.

Luxury: To indulge in luxury, Lisbon has exceptional five-star hotels like Four Seasons Hotel Ritz Lisbon,

Pestana Palace Lisbon, and Bairro Alto Hotel, offering top-notch service and stunning views.

Porto:

Budget: Porto has several budget-friendly accommodations, particularly in the city center and Ribeira district. Some options include Gallery Hostel, Tattva Design Hostel, and Porto Lounge Hostel.

Mid-range: Porto offers a range of mid-range hotels like Hotel Mercure Porto Centro, Moov Hotel Porto Centro, and Porto A.S. 1829 Hotel, which provide a comfortable stay with reasonable prices.

Luxury: For luxury experiences, consider hotels such as The Yeatman, InterContinental Porto - Palacio das Cardosas, or Pestana Vintage Porto Hotel & World Heritage Site, which offer exceptional service and upscale amenities.

Algarve:

Budget: In the Algarve region, particularly in cities like Albufeira and Lagos, you can find affordable accommodations such as Albufeira Lounge Guesthouse, Lagos City Center Guest House & Hostel, or Lagosmar Hotel.

Mid-range: For mid-range options in the Algarve, consider hotels like Tivoli Lagos, Vila Petra, or Hotel Vila Galé Praia, which offer comfortable stays and convenient locations.

Luxury: The Algarve boasts several luxurious resorts and hotels. Some noteworthy choices include Anantara Vilamoura Algarve Resort, Pine Cliffs Hotel - a Luxury Collection Resort, and Conrad Algarve, providing upscale amenities, stunning views, and impeccable service.

Madeira:

Budget: Madeira offers affordable accommodations such as Residencial Americana, Residencial Colombo, or Residencial Funchal, providing comfortable stays at reasonable prices.

Mid-range: Consider mid-range options like Porto Mare Hotel, Pestana Carlton Madeira, or Quinta da Casa Branca for a pleasant stay with additional amenities.

Luxury: Madeira is home to luxurious hotels like Belmond Reid's Palace, The Cliff Bay, and Vidamar Resort Hotel Madeira, which offer high-end experiences, beautiful locations, and excellent facilities.

Remember to consider factors like location, accessibility, and proximity to attractions when choosing your accommodation in Portugal. Prices may vary depending on the season, so it's recommended to book in advance for better deals.

Tips on the best places to stay

When considering the best places to stay in Portugal, here are some tips to help you make the most informed decision:

Lisbon: The capital city of Portugal, Lisbon offers a vibrant atmosphere, historic sites, and a wide range of accommodations. Consider staying in the neighborhoods of Baixa, Alfama, Chiado, or Bairro Alto for easy access to attractions, restaurants, and nightlife.

Porto: Known for its charming old town and port wine, Porto is a popular destination in Portugal. Look for accommodations in the Ribeira district or near

Avenida dos Aliados to be close to the main sights and the Douro River.

Algarve: If you're seeking beautiful beaches and resort towns, the Algarve region is a top choice. Consider staying in cities like Albufeira, Lagos, Vilamoura, or Faro, which offer a variety of accommodations and easy access to stunning coastal areas.

Madeira: The picturesque island of Madeira is a great option for nature lovers and outdoor enthusiasts. Funchal, the capital, offers a range of accommodations, while quieter areas like Santana and Calheta provide a more serene setting.

Sintra: Just a short distance from Lisbon, Sintra is known for its fairytale-like palaces and enchanting forests. Consider staying in the town center to explore attractions such as Pena Palace, Quinta da Regaleira, and the Moorish Castle.

Douro Valley: For wine enthusiasts and those seeking a tranquil countryside experience, the Douro Valley is a fantastic choice. Look for accommodations in towns like Peso da Régua or Pinhão, where you can enjoy vineyard views and take scenic river cruises.

Évora: Located in the Alentejo region, Évora is a UNESCO World Heritage site with well-preserved Roman ruins and a charming old town. Stay in the historic center to be close to attractions like the Roman Temple, the Cathedral, and the Bone Chapel.

Cascais: Situated on the Lisbon coast, Cascais is a popular beach destination with a lively atmosphere. Consider staying near the town center or along the Estoril Coast for easy access to the beach, shops, and restaurants.

Aveiro: Known as the "Venice of Portugal," Aveiro is famous for its canals, colorful Moliceiro boats, and Art Nouveau architecture. Stay in the city center to explore the canals, visit Aveiro's beaches, and try the local cuisine.

Coimbra: Home to one of Europe's oldest universities, Coimbra offers a rich history and a vibrant student atmosphere. Stay near the university or in the city center to explore the historic sites, museums, and lively nightlife.

When choosing accommodations, consider factors such as your budget, preferred location, proximity to attractions, and the type of experience you're seeking. Additionally, booking in advance is recommended, especially during peak travel seasons, to secure the best options and rates.

Chapter 7.
Activities to do as a family

Portugal offers a variety of family-friendly activities that cater to children of all ages. Here are some engaging activities to consider during your trip:

- Visit Oceanário de Lisboa (Lisbon): Explore the Oceanário de Lisboa, one of the largest aquariums in Europe. Children can marvel at a diverse range of marine life, including sharks, penguins, and colorful fish. The interactive exhibits and educational programs make it an exciting and educational experience for the whole family.
- Explore KidZania (Lisbon): KidZania is an interactive indoor theme park in Lisbon where children can role-play different professions, such as doctors, firefighters, or chefs. It's a

hands-on learning experience that promotes creativity, teamwork, and independence.

- Enjoy the beaches: Portugal has beautiful beaches suitable for families, such as Praia da Rocha (Algarve), Praia da Figueira (Sintra), or Praia de Carcavelos (Cascais). Spend a day building sandcastles, swimming in the sea, and soaking up the sun. Many beaches have facilities like lifeguards and beachfront restaurants.
- Visit the Lisbon Zoo: Take your children to the Lisbon Zoo (Jardim Zoológico de Lisboa) where they can encounter a wide range of animals from different continents. The zoo offers educational shows, interactive exhibits, and a petting zoo, allowing kids to have an up-close experience with wildlife.
- Explore the Science Museum (Porto): The Science Museum (Museu de Ciência do Porto) in Porto is an interactive space where children can learn about science through engaging exhibits and experiments. It's a fantastic place to stimulate curiosity and inspire young minds.
- Discover the theme parks: Portugal is home to several theme parks that offer a fun-filled day for families. Consider visiting places like Zoomarine (Algarve) with its dolphin shows and water slides, or Portugal dos Pequenitos (Coimbra) that showcases scaled-down replicas of Portuguese monuments and cultural exhibits.
- Explore the Pena Park and Palace (Sintra): Take a family hike in the beautiful Pena Park, surrounding the colorful Pena Palace. The park offers picturesque trails, hidden

pathways, and breathtaking views. Children will enjoy the fairytale-like atmosphere and exploring the palace's nooks and crannies.

- Ride the historic tram (Lisbon): Hop on the historic Tram 28 in Lisbon for a scenic ride through narrow streets and steep hills. Kids will enjoy the vintage charm of the tram while experiencing the city's vibrant neighborhoods like Alfama and Graça.
- Discover the theme park and wax museum: Visit Portugal dos Pequenitos (Coimbra), a park dedicated to showcasing Portugal's culture, history, and architecture in miniature form. Next to the park, you'll find the wax museum Museu de Cera, featuring lifelike wax figures of historical and cultural icons.
- Enjoy water sports: Portugal's coastline offers opportunities for water sports suitable for families. Try activities like paddleboarding, kayaking, or taking a family surf lesson. Locations like Cascais, Lagos, or Peniche provide ideal conditions and equipment rentals for these activities.

Remember to consider the age and interests of your children when planning activities. It's also a good idea to check the opening hours, availability, and any age restrictions or safety guidelines for each activity or attraction you plan to visit.

Chapter 8.
Transportation, buses and cabs

Transportation in Portugal is well-developed, offering various options for getting around cities and traveling between different regions. Portugal has an extensive and efficient train network that connects major cities and towns throughout the country. The trains in Portugal are operated by Comboios de Portugal (CP), the national railway company.

Trains

Here are the main types of trains you can find in Portugal:

- Alfa Pendular: Alfa Pendular is the flagship high-speed train service in Portugal. It connects major cities such as Lisbon, Porto, Braga, Guimarães, Coimbra, and Faro. These trains offer comfortable seating, onboard amenities like Wi-Fi, power outlets, and a bar/buffet car. Alfa Pendular trains can reach speeds of up to 220 km/h (137 mph), making them the fastest option for long-distance travel within the country.

- Intercidades: Intercidades trains provide an efficient and comfortable service connecting major cities and towns in Portugal. They offer both first and second-class seating, with amenities such as power outlets and air conditioning. Intercidades trains operate on both high-speed lines and traditional lines, allowing passengers to reach destinations like Lisbon, Porto, Évora, Guarda, Covilhã, and others.

- Regional and InterRegional: Regional and InterRegional trains are slower, stopping at more stations, and are mainly used for shorter distances and local travel. They connect smaller towns and villages with larger cities, providing an important transportation link for local communities. These trains offer second-class seating and have fewer amenities compared to the high-speed trains.

- Urban Trains: Portugal also has urban train services that operate within major metropolitan areas. In Lisbon, there is the CP Urban Services that connect the city center with suburban areas and neighboring towns. Porto has its own urban train network called Metro do Porto, which provides transportation within the city and surrounding areas.

- International Trains: Portugal is well connected to its neighboring countries by train. There are international train services that connect Lisbon and Porto with cities in Portugal, including Madrid and Vigo. These trains are operated by the Spanish railway company Renfe.

It's important to note that train services and schedules may be subject to change, so it's advisable to check the latest information on the official website of Comboios de Portugal or consult local travel resources before planning your trip.

Here's an overview of the transportation systems, including metro lines, buses, and cabs, and how they work in Portugal:

Metro Lines:

Lisbon Metro: Lisbon has a reliable and efficient metro system that serves the city and surrounding areas. It consists of four lines (Blue, Yellow, Green, and Red) that cover major neighborhoods, tourist attractions, and transportation hubs. The metro operates from around 6:30 am until 1:00 am, and tickets can be purchased at the stations or using rechargeable cards.

Porto Metro: Porto also has a metro system that connects the city and its suburbs. It has six lines (A, B, C, D, E, and F) that provide convenient transportation. The metro operates from around 6:00 am until 1:00 am, and tickets can be purchased at the stations or using rechargeable Andante cards.

Cabs:

Taxis: Taxis are widely available in cities and towns throughout Portugal. They can be hailed on the street, found at designated taxi stands, or booked through phone apps. Taxis in Portugal are generally metered, and it's advisable to ensure the driver starts the meter at the beginning of the trip. Uber and other ride-sharing services are also available in major cities.

Tipping: It is customary to round up the fare or add a small tip, typically around 5% to 10% of the total amount.

It's important to note that public transportation systems in Portugal typically operate on a schedule, and it's a good idea to check the timetables in advance, especially for early morning or late-night travel. Additionally, purchasing rechargeable cards like Viva Viagem (Lisbon) or Andante (Porto) can offer convenience and cost savings for frequent travelers.

Buses:

City Buses: Both Lisbon and Porto have extensive bus networks that cover the entire city and its outskirts. Buses operate from early morning until around midnight, depending on the route. Tickets can be purchased on the bus or using rechargeable cards like Viva Viagem (Lisbon) or Andante (Porto).

Intercity Buses: Portugal has a comprehensive network of intercity buses that connect major cities and towns across the country. Companies like Rede Expressos and FlixBus offer comfortable and affordable options for traveling longer distances. Tickets can be purchased online or at bus stations.

How to move easily to see the main attractions for each city

Portugal offers a variety of attractions that can be easily reached by bus, providing a convenient and cost-effective way to explore the country. Here are some of the main attractions in Portugal and information on how to reach them by bus, along with links to relevant bus companies where you can purchase tickets:

Lisbon:

Lisbon, the capital city of Portugal, is a vibrant destination with numerous attractions. To get around Lisbon, you can use the local public transportation system, including buses, trams, and the metro. Carris is the main bus company in Lisbon, and you can find routes and timetables on their website: Carris website. Lisbon also offers hop-on hop-off bus tours, which are a convenient way to visit the city's major sights. You can check out companies like Yellow Bus or City Sightseeing Lisbon for these tours.

In Lisbon, one of the most convenient ways to explore the city and reach its main attractions is by using the hop-on-hop-off bus service. This type of bus allows you to hop on and off at various stops throughout the city, giving you the flexibility to visit the attractions that interest you the most. Here are some key points about the bus service and the stops that are within easy reach of the main attractions in Lisbon:

Hop-on-Hop-off Bus Service: There are several hop-on-hop-off bus companies operating in Lisbon, such as Yellow Bus and City Sightseeing Lisbon. These buses typically follow specific routes that cover the major tourist areas and attractions in the city.

Key Stops: The bus routes in Lisbon usually include stops at popular attractions, historical sites, and scenic viewpoints. Some of the key stops you might encounter while using the hop-on-hop-off bus service in Lisbon are:

- Praça do Comércio: Located near the waterfront, this square is a great starting point to explore Lisbon. From here, you can walk to the Alfama district, the Lisbon Cathedral, and other nearby attractions.
- Rossio Square: Situated in the heart of the city, Rossio Square is surrounded by shops, cafes, and historic buildings. It is within walking distance of the Baixa-Chiado district and close to the Elevador de Santa Justa, a popular viewpoint.
- Belém Tower: This iconic tower is a UNESCO World Heritage Site and a must-visit attraction in Lisbon. It is located in the Belém neighborhood and is easily accessible from the bus stops nearby.
- Jerónimos Monastery: Another UNESCO World Heritage Site, the Jerónimos Monastery is also situated in Belém. It is renowned for its impressive Manueline architecture and is close to the Belém Tower.
- Parque das Nações: This modern area of Lisbon was revitalized for the World Expo '98. It features attractions like the Oceanarium, cable car rides, and riverside promenades. The bus stops here provide easy access to this vibrant district.
- Castelo de São Jorge: Perched on a hill, the São Jorge Castle offers panoramic views of the city. The bus may stop nearby, allowing you to explore the castle and its surroundings.
- Audio Commentary: Hop-on-hop-off buses typically provide multilingual audio commentary on board, offering information about the attractions and landmarks you pass

along the way. This enhances your understanding and appreciation of the city's history and culture.

- Flexibility and Convenience: The hop-on-hop-off bus service in Lisbon allows you to tailor your itinerary according to your interests and available time. You can explore each attraction at your own pace and catch the next bus when you're ready to move on.

It's important to note that the availability of specific bus routes, stops, and attractions may vary depending on the hop-on-hop-off bus company and the current circumstances. It's advisable to check the routes and schedules in advance to plan your sightseeing effectively.

Overall, the hop-on-hop-off bus service in Lisbon provides a convenient and efficient way to visit the city's main attractions. It offers flexibility, informative commentary, and easy access to popular landmarks, making it an excellent option for tourists wanting to explore Lisbon's highlights.

Porto:

Porto, located in the north of Portugal, is known for its charming old town, historic port wine cellars, and the iconic Dom Luís I Bridge. STCP is the primary bus company operating in Porto. You can find information about routes, schedules, and fares on their website: STCP website. Additionally, Porto has a hop-on hop-off sightseeing bus service operated by Porto Vintage.

The local public transportation system, including buses, is well-developed and offers a convenient way to get around. Here's some information about the buses in Porto and the stops that are within easy reach of the city's main attractions:

- Public Bus Service: The public bus service in Porto is operated by the company STCP (Sociedade de Transportes Colectivos do Porto). They have an extensive network of bus routes that cover the city and its surroundings.
- Key Stops and Attractions: Porto's main attractions are spread across the city, and there are bus stops conveniently located near many of them. Here are some of the main attractions and the nearby bus stops:

1. Ribeira: The historic district of Ribeira, with its colorful houses and riverside promenade, is a popular tourist area. The bus lines 500 and 900 stop nearby, allowing you to explore this charming neighborhood.
2. Torre dos Clérigos: The Clérigos Tower is one of Porto's iconic landmarks. It's situated near the city center, and buses that stop nearby include lines 300, 301, and 602.
3. Livraria Lello: This famous bookstore, known for its stunning architecture, is located close to the Clérigos Tower. Bus lines 300, 301, and 602 also stop nearby, making it easily accessible.
4. São Bento Station: Known for its beautiful azulejo tilework, São Bento Station is a transportation hub and a sightseeing spot in itself. Many bus lines pass by or have stops near the station, including lines 200, 201, and 207.
5. Casa da Música: This contemporary concert hall is an architectural gem. It's situated a bit outside the city center but is easily accessible

by bus. Bus lines 204, 504, and 601 are among those that serve this area.

6. Matosinhos Beach: If you wish to visit the beach, Matosinhos is a popular choice. Bus lines 500, 507, and 508 connect Porto with Matosinhos, allowing you to enjoy the sandy shores and seafood restaurants.

- Andante Card: To use the public buses in Porto, it's recommended to purchase an Andante Card, which is a rechargeable transportation card. You can load it with credit and use it for multiple journeys on various modes of transportation, including buses, trams, and the metro.

- Timetables and Schedules: Bus timetables and schedules can vary, so it's advisable to check the STCP website or use public transportation apps to plan your journey and stay updated on bus times.

The public bus service in Porto offers an efficient way to visit the city's main attractions. While the buses don't typically provide guided commentary like hop-on-hop-off buses, they offer a more cost-effective and flexible option for getting around. With the convenience of bus stops near key attractions, you can easily explore Porto's highlights and immerse yourself in its rich culture and history.

Sintra:

Sintra is a picturesque town near Lisbon, famous for its fairy-tale-like castles and palaces, including Pena Palace and Quinta da Regaleira. To reach Sintra from Lisbon, you can take a train from Rossio Station or a bus from Sete Rios Bus Station. Scotturb is the bus company that operates the main routes in Sintra.

Sintra is known for its fairytale palaces, enchanting gardens, and historical sites. Here's some information about the buses in Sintra and the stops that are within easy reach of the town's main attractions:

- Scotturb Bus Service: The primary bus company operating in Sintra is Scotturb. They provide regular bus services that connect the town center with the various attractions in the area.
- Key Stops and Attractions: Sintra is home to several notable attractions, and the bus stops are strategically placed near these sites. Here are some of the main attractions and the nearby bus stops:
1. Sintra National Palace: Located in the heart of the town, the Sintra National Palace is one of the most iconic landmarks. It is easily accessible from the main bus terminal in Sintra, known as "Estação de Autocarros," which is the central hub for bus services.
2. Quinta da Regaleira: This mystical estate features lush gardens, underground tunnels, and a romantic palace. The bus lines 435 and 435T connect the town center with Quinta da Regaleira.
3. Pena Palace: One of the most enchanting palaces in Sintra, the Pena Palace sits atop a hill, surrounded by lush forests. To reach the palace, you can take the bus lines 434 or 434T from the town center.
4. Moorish Castle: Situated near the Pena Palace, the Moorish Castle offers panoramic views of the surrounding area. Bus line 434 or 434T can take you to the entrance of the castle.

5. Monserrate Palace: Known for its stunning architecture and extensive gardens, Monserrate Palace is a hidden gem in Sintra. Bus lines 435 or 435T provide service to Monserrate.

- Timetables and Schedules: It's important to check the bus timetables and schedules in advance, as they may vary depending on the time of year and day of the week. Scotturb's website or the local tourist information center can provide up-to-date information on bus routes and schedules.

- Tickets and Payment: You can purchase bus tickets directly from the bus driver upon boarding. It's advisable to have cash on hand, as not all buses accept card payments. Alternatively, you can consider purchasing a rechargeable transportation card, such as the Viva Viagem card, in Lisbon, which can be used on Sintra's buses as well.

The bus service in Sintra offers a practical way to explore the town and visit its main attractions. While the bus routes do not typically offer guided commentary, they provide an affordable and efficient means of transportation. With the convenient bus stops located near the key attractions, you can easily immerse yourself in the magical atmosphere of Sintra and experience its architectural wonders and natural beauty.

Évora:

Évora is a UNESCO World Heritage site located in the Alentejo region of Portugal. It is known for its well-preserved medieval walls, Roman Temple, and the impressive Cathedral of Évora. Rede Expressos is the main long-distance bus company in Portugal and offers connections to Évora from various cities, including Lisbon.

Here's some information about the buses in Évora and the stops that are within easy reach of the city's main attractions:

- Local Bus Service: The local bus service in Évora is operated by a company called TUD - Transportes Urbanos de Évora. They provide regular bus routes that cover the city and its surrounding areas.
- Key Stops and Attractions: Évora boasts numerous attractions, and the bus stops are conveniently located near many of them. Here are some of the main attractions and the nearby bus stops:
1. Praça do Giraldo: This central square is the heart of Évora and a great starting point for exploration. It is well-connected by various bus routes, and several buses stop here.
2. Cathedral of Évora (Sé de Évora): The impressive Évora Cathedral is within easy walking distance from Praça do Giraldo, and there are bus stops nearby if you prefer to take the bus.
3. Templo Romano (Roman Temple): This ancient Roman temple is a significant landmark in Évora. It is located near the city center, and buses that pass through Praça do Giraldo, such as bus lines 1, 2, 4, and 6, can take you close to the temple.
4. Capela dos Ossos (Chapel of Bones): Known for its macabre interior adorned with human bones, the Chapel of Bones is located near the

Church of St. Francis. Bus lines 2 and 4 can take you to the area.

5. University of Évora: The historic University of Évora is worth a visit. Bus lines 1, 2, 4, and 6 have stops near the university, making it easily accessible.

6. Aqueduto da Água de Prata (Silver Water Aqueduct): This impressive aqueduct, which dates back to the 16th century, is located outside the city walls. Bus line 2 can take you to the area near the aqueduct.

-   Timetables and Schedules: Bus timetables and schedules in Évora may vary depending on the route and the day of the week. It's advisable to check the TUD website or contact the local tourist information center for up-to-date information on bus routes and schedules.

-   Tickets and Payment: Bus tickets can be purchased directly from the bus driver upon boarding. Cash is usually accepted, but having small change is recommended. Some buses may also accept contactless card payments, but it's always a good idea to carry cash as a backup.

Faro and Algarve:

Faro is the gateway to the Algarve region, which is famous for its stunning beaches and coastal scenery. Eva Transportes is a major bus company serving the Algarve, with connections to cities like Faro, Lagos, Albufeira, and others.

In Faro and the Algarve region of Portugal, the local bus service is an efficient and reliable way to explore the area and visit the main attractions. Here's some information about the buses in Faro and the Algarve, along with the stops that are within easy reach of the region's key attractions:

- EVA Transportes: The primary bus company operating in Faro and the Algarve is EVA Transportes. They provide extensive bus services that connect various towns, cities, and attractions in the region.
- Key Stops and Attractions: The Algarve is known for its stunning beaches, charming towns, and picturesque landscapes. Here are some main attractions and the nearby bus stops:

1. Faro Old Town: The historic center of Faro, with its cobbled streets and medieval architecture, is worth exploring. The bus station in Faro is centrally located, and you can easily access the Old Town and its attractions on foot.
2. Praia de Faro: This popular beach is located on a sandbar, accessible by bridge from Faro. Bus lines 14 and 16 provide direct service from Faro to Praia de Faro.
3. Albufeira: Known for its lively nightlife and beautiful beaches, Albufeira is a major tourist destination. Buses run regularly between Faro and Albufeira, with the journey taking around 45 minutes to an hour.
4. Lagos: This historic town offers stunning coastal scenery, charming streets, and nearby attractions like Ponta da Piedade. Buses connect Faro and Lagos, with a travel time of approximately two hours.
5. Vilamoura: This upscale resort town is known for its marina, golf courses, and luxury hotels.

Bus lines connect Faro and Vilamoura, with a journey time of around 30-40 minutes.

6. Sagres: Located at the southwestern tip of Portugal, Sagres offers breathtaking cliffs, beautiful beaches, and historical sites like the Fortaleza de Sagres. Buses run from Faro to Sagres, with a journey time of around three hours.

- Timetables and Schedules: Bus timetables and schedules can vary depending on the route, the season, and the day of the week. It's advisable to check the EVA Transportes website or consult local information sources for the most up-to-date schedules.
- Tickets and Payment: Bus tickets can be purchased directly from the bus driver upon boarding. It's recommended to have cash on hand for ticket purchases, as not all buses accept card payments.

The bus service in Faro and the Algarve offers a convenient way to explore the region's main attractions. While the travel times between certain destinations may be longer, the buses provide a comfortable and affordable option for sightseeing. With the well-connected bus network and easily accessible stops, you can enjoy the stunning beaches, historic towns, and natural beauty that the Algarve has to offer.

Coimbra:

Coimbra, located in central Portugal, is home to one of the oldest universities in the world and offers a rich history and cultural heritage. Rede Expressos and FlixBus are two bus companies that provide connections to Coimbra.

Here's some information about the buses in Coimbra and the stops that are within easy reach of the city's key attractions:

- SMTUC (Sociedade de Transportes Urbanos de Coimbra): The primary bus company operating in Coimbra is SMTUC. They provide comprehensive bus services that cover the city and its surrounding areas.
- Key Stops and Attractions: Coimbra boasts several notable attractions, and the bus stops are conveniently located near many of them. Here are some main attractions and the nearby bus stops:

1. University of Coimbra: One of the oldest universities in Europe, the University of Coimbra is a UNESCO World Heritage Site. The bus lines 1, 34, and 38 take you close to the university campus.
2. Sé Velha (Old Cathedral): This medieval cathedral is a prominent landmark in Coimbra. Bus lines 1, 5, 11, 12, 24, and 36 can take you to stops near the cathedral.
3. Portugal dos Pequenitos: A popular family attraction, Portugal dos Pequenitos is a miniature park representing Portugal's architectural landmarks. Bus lines 34 and 37 provide service to this attraction.
4. Santa Clara-a-Velha Monastery: Located on the banks of the Mondego River, this ruined monastery is an atmospheric historical site. Bus lines 34 and 37 pass by the area.
5. Baixa (Downtown): Coimbra's downtown area is a vibrant district with shops, cafes, and historical buildings. Several bus lines,

including 5, 6, 7, 11, 24, and 37, serve stops in the downtown area.

6. Convento de Santa Clara-a-Nova (Santa Clara-a-Nova Monastery): Situated on a hill overlooking the city, this monastery offers panoramic views of Coimbra. Bus lines 6, 7, and 37 can take you to the vicinity of the monastery.

- Timetables and Schedules: Bus timetables and schedules may vary depending on the route and the day of the week. It's advisable to check the SMTUC website or consult local information sources for the most up-to-date schedules.

- Tickets and Payment: Bus tickets can be purchased directly from the bus driver upon boarding. It's recommended to have cash on hand for ticket purchases, as not all buses accept card payments.

Overall, public transportation in Portugal is generally reliable, efficient, and cost-effective, providing convenient options for exploring cities and traveling between different regions of the country.

Chapter 9.
Travel seasons

What to pack for a trip to Portugal will depend on the season and specific activities you plan to engage in. Portugal generally experiences mild winters and hot summers, but there can be regional variations. Here are some general packing recommendations based on the seasons:

Spring (March to May) and Autumn (September to November):

Lightweight clothing: Pack a mix of long and short-sleeved shirts, lightweight pants, and skirts or dresses. Layering is key during these transitional seasons.

Light jacket or sweater: Mornings and evenings can be cooler, so having a light jacket or sweater is advisable.

Comfortable walking shoes: Portugal offers plenty of opportunities for walking and exploring, so bring comfortable footwear for sightseeing.

Rain gear: Spring and autumn can have occasional rain showers, so pack a compact umbrella or a waterproof jacket.

Summer (June to August):

Lightweight and breathable clothing: Pack light, breathable fabrics such as cotton and linen. T-shirts, shorts, dresses, and skirts are suitable for the hot weather.

Swimwear: Portugal has beautiful beaches, so don't forget to bring swimwear and a beach towel.

Sun protection: Bring sunscreen, sunglasses, and a hat to protect yourself from the strong summer sun.

Sandals or flip-flops: Comfortable and breathable footwear is essential for warm weather.

Winter (December to February):

Warm clothing: Portugal's winters are generally mild, but it's advisable to bring some warm layers. Include sweaters, long-sleeved shirts, pants, and a coat or jacket.

Scarf, hat, and gloves: For cooler mornings and evenings, pack accessories to keep yourself warm.

Umbrella: Rain showers are more common in winter, so having a compact umbrella or a waterproof jacket is recommended.

Closed-toe shoes: Choose comfortable shoes suitable for colder weather and occasional rain.

Other essential items to pack regardless of the season:

Travel adapter: Portugal uses the Europlug (Type C) and Schuko (Type F) power outlets, so bring a suitable adapter if needed.

Travel documents: Don't forget to bring your passport, travel insurance, and any necessary visas or ID cards.

Medications: If you take any prescription medications, ensure you have an adequate supply for your trip.

Portable charger: A portable charger will come in handy for keeping your devices charged while you're out and about.

Daypack or tote bag: Bring a small bag to carry essentials during day trips and excursions.

Remember to check the weather forecast for your specific travel dates and the regions you plan to visit. This will help you pack accordingly and ensure you are prepared for the local conditions.

Portuguese language basics

Greetings:

- Olá! (Hello!)
- Bom dia! (Good morning!)
- Boa tarde! (Good afternoon!)
- Boa noite! (Good evening/night!)

Polite phrases:

- Por favor (Please)
- Obrigado (male) / Obrigada (female) (Thank you)
- Desculpe (Excuse me/sorry)
- Com licença (Excuse me)

Basic conversation:

- Como está? (How are you?)
- Tudo bem? (Everything good?)
- Fala inglês? (Do you speak English?)
- Não entendo (I don't understand)

- Falo um pouco de português (I speak a little Portuguese)

Ordering food and drinks:

- Quero (I want)
- Por favor, um café (Please, a coffee)
- Quanto custa? (How much does it cost?)
- A conta, por favor (The bill, please)

Getting around:

- Onde fica...? (Where is...?)
- À esquerda (To the left)
- À direita (To the right)
- Estou perdido(a) (I'm lost)
- Pode me ajudar? (Can you help me?)

Common expressions:

- Muito prazer (Nice to meet you)
- Não tem problema (No problem)
- Estou com fome (I'm hungry)
- Estou com sede (I'm thirsty)
- Tenha um bom dia (Have a good day)

Portuguese dialect expressions (specific to Portugal):

- Fixe (Cool/nice)
- Bicho (Dude/guy)
- Tas a ver? (You know?)
- Está tudo bem? (Is everything okay?)
- Ficar à toa (To do nothing/laze around)

Common expressions:

Fogo! (Wow!/Geez!)

Estou a ver (I see/I understand)

Está bem (Okay/alright)

Não faz mal (It's okay/never mind)

Não sei (I don't know)

Ordering in a restaurant:

Uma mesa para [número de pessoas], por favor (A table for [number of people], please)

Eu gostaria de experimentar [prato típico] (I would like to try [typical dish])

Que recomenda? (What do you recommend?)

Mais uma cerveja/vinho, por favor (One more beer/wine, please)

Shopping:

Quanto custa? (How much does it cost?)

Posso experimentar isso? (Can I try this?)

Aceita cartão de crédito? (Do you accept credit cards?)

Tem algum desconto? (Is there any discount?)

Transportation:

Onde é a estação de comboios/autocarros? (Where is the train/bus station?)

Quanto custa um bilhete para [destino]? (How much is a ticket to [destination]?)

A que horas parte o próximo comboio/autocarro para [destino]? (What time does the next train/bus leave for [destination]?)

Preciso de um táxi (I need a taxi)

Emergencies:

Ajuda! (Help!)

Onde fica o hospital/telefone? (Where is the hospital/telephone?)

Perdi a minha carteira/passaporte (I lost my wallet/passport)

Preciso de um médico (I need a doctor)

Remember that these phrases are specific to European Portuguese, as spoken in Portugal. The pronunciation and some vocabulary might differ slightly from Brazilian Portuguese. Learning a few basic phrases will help you communicate and connect with locals during your trip.

Chapter 10.
The currency exchange and which foreign ATMs to use

When traveling to Portugal, it's important to have an understanding of currency exchange and find ways to minimize fees and risks associated with using foreign ATMs. Here are some tips to consider:

- Currency in Portugal: The official currency in Portugal is the Euro (€). It is advisable to exchange your currency to Euros before your trip, either at your local bank or a reputable currency exchange service. It's generally recommended to carry a mix of cash and use cards for convenience.

- Exchanging Currency: Banks and official currency exchange offices typically offer competitive rates. Avoid exchanging money at airports or touristy areas, as they often charge higher fees or less favorable exchange rates.

- ATMs in Portugal: ATMs (known as "Multibancos" in Portugal) are widely available throughout the country and are a convenient way to withdraw cash. Look for ATMs affiliated with major banks, such as Millennium BCP, Caixa Geral de Depósitos, or Santander, as they tend to have more favorable exchange rates and lower fees.
- Avoid Dynamic Currency Conversion (DCC): When using your credit card at merchants or ATMs, you may encounter the option for Dynamic Currency Conversion. This allows you to pay in your home currency, but it often comes with higher fees and unfavorable exchange rates. Always choose to be charged in the local currency (Euros) to avoid excessive charges.
- Notify Your Bank: Prior to your trip, inform your bank or credit card provider about your travel plans. This helps avoid any unexpected card blocks due to suspicious activity when using your cards abroad.

ATM Safety Tips: To minimize the risk of fraud or criminal activity at ATMs, keep the following precautions in mind:

- Use ATMs located in well-lit and secure areas, preferably inside banks or reputable establishments.
- Shield your PIN entry with your hand or body to prevent it from being seen by others.
- Be cautious of anyone offering assistance or acting suspiciously around the ATM.

- Regularly monitor your bank statements for any unauthorized transactions.
- Additional Payment Options: Credit cards, especially those with no foreign transaction fees, are widely accepted in most establishments in Portugal. It's a convenient and secure way to make payments. However, it's always good to carry some cash for small expenses or places that may not accept cards.

Remember to research and compare fees and exchange rates offered by your specific bank or financial institution to ensure you make the most cost-effective choices during your trip to Portugal.

Conclusion

This travel guide is structured into a series of sections that provide valuable information. It is a reliable and comprehensive resource, offering practical information, expert recommendations, and helpful tips that simplify travel arrangements. It empowers travelers with the knowledge and tools to plan an itinerary, navigate the country, and make the most of their time in Portugal. By leveraging the insights, a travel guide provides, individuals can optimize their travel experiences, avoid unnecessary stress, and create cherished memories of their visit to this vibrant and diverse country.

This guide is intended for all travelers to Portugal, whether on business or pleasure, whether for a one- or two-week visit. Thank you for reading this complete guide on Portugal, a country that will make you fall in love with its variety and charm. With the information we have provided you, you can start planning your trip in complete autonomy and safety, choosing the destinations that interest you most and the activities that you like best. Whether you are looking for relaxation, adventure, art or gastronomy, Portugal has something to offer you in every season of the year. Don't miss the opportunity to discover its beauties and traditions, to taste its typical dishes and wines, to meet its hospitable and cheerful people. Portugal awaits you with open arms to give you an unforgettable experience. Are you ready to leave? Pack your bags and get ready to live a dream. Portugal will surprise you with its colors, its scents, its sounds and its emotions. Have a good trip!

References:

images: Freepik.com.

The images within this book were chosen using resources from Freepik.com

Made in the USA
Las Vegas, NV
09 June 2023

73159646R10081